Our Small Planet

Our small planet is getting endangered: by the arsenals of weapons which could blow it up; by the burden of military expenditures which could sink it under; and by the unmet basic needs of two-thirds of its population which subsists on less than one-third of its resources. We belong to a near universal constituency which believes that we are borrowing this Earth from our children as much as we have inherited it from our forefathers. The carrying capacity of Earth is not infinite, nor are its resources. The needs of national security are legitimate and must be met. But must we stand by as helpless witnesses of a drift towards greater insecurity at higher cost?

– Joint Declaration by Panel of Eminent Persons advising the International Conference on the Relationship between Disarmament and Development:

Inga Thorsson; Sweden, (Moderator)
Ibrahim Hilmy Abdel-Rahman, Egypt
Tamas Bacskai, Hungary
Oleg T. Bogomolov, USSR
Gamani Corea, Sri Lanka
Edgar Faure, France
Alfonso Garcia-Robles, Mexico
Lawrence Klein, U.S.
Pei Monong, China
Raul Prebisch, Argentina
Walter Scheel, Federal Republic of Germany
Agha Shahi, Pakistan
Janez Stanovnik, Yugoslavia

New York, 1986

For my children,

Evita, Michaelene, Douglas Francis, Mary Anne, Patricia

Books By Douglas Roche

The Catholic Revolution, 1968.

Man to Man (with Bishop Remi De Roo), 1969.

It's a New World, 1970.

Justice Not Charity: A New Global Ethic for Canada, 1976.

The Human Side of Politics, 1976.

What Development Is All About, 1979.

Politicians for Peace, 1983.

United Nations: Divided World, 1984.

Building Global Security:

Agenda for the 1990's

Douglas Roche

Foreword by Maurice Strong

NC Press Limited

Toronto, 1989

Canadian Cataloguing in Publication Data

Roche, Douglas, 1929-
    Building Global Security

Includes bibliographical references.
ISBN 1-55021-057-2

1. World politics - 1985-1995. 2. Social problems.
3. International relations. I. Title.

HN17.5.R2 1989   909.82'9   C89-09859-3

New Canada Publications, a division of NC Press Limited,
Box 452, Station A, Toronto, Ontario, Canada, M5W 1H8.

Printed and bound in Canada

Contents

Acknowledgments

This book is the product of many years of reflection during my careers as a journalist, parliamentarian and diplomat. I have had a privileged position in being able to see so many sides of the world, from the villages of Bangladesh to the working rooms of the United Nations. I cannot name here all who have influenced my thinking, but three persons taught me how to see the planet Earth: the philosopher Jacques Maritain, the development economist Barbara Ward, the U.N. expert Robert Muller.

Maurice Strong, who has made Canada's name shine in United Nation's environment and development activities for 20 years, honoured me by writing the Foreword.

The facts in this book are rooted in United Nations' documentation. In writing it, I received special assistance from the Canadian Centre for Arms Control and Disarmament. The executive director, John Lamb provided valuable insights and criticism. Jane Boulden assisted me with research. Helene Haddad and Gemma Idurot prepared the manuscript. I am grateful to all my friends at the Centre.

Robert Miller, Associate, Parliamentary Centre for Foreign Affairs and Foreign Trade, offered, as he has with my previous books, beneficial advice. Jim LeBlanc made helpful suggestions.

My publisher, NC Press, provided guidance and I thank especialy Caroline Walker and Norman Endicott.

While all who read and commented on the manuscript helped to improve it, the final responsibility remains, as it must, with the author.

Douglas Roche

Edmonton

Foreword

By Maurice Strong

Security has always been a central preoccupation of individuals and of states. It has traditionally been equated with possession of the military strength needed to deter or defend against aggression. But today, in our increasingly complex and interdependent world, threats to the survival of people and nations can also arise from ecological, economic and social vulnerability.

Each of these risks is related to one other in various ways through a complex system of interacting relationships that is increasingly global in its scale and context. Thus, no nation today can ensure the security of its people by its own actions alone. National security can only be achieved by ensuring global security. And this can only be accomplished by cooperation among the nations of the world to an extent and in ways which go well beyond anything yet experienced.

There has been a dramatic improvement in the climate for international cooperation as a result of the thaw in the Cold War and the dynamics of *perestroika*. This opens up the exciting new prospects for building global security in the decade of the 1990's to which this important and timely book is addressed.

While our history has been shaped and our values debased by war, the achievement of peace has been one of mankind's most enduring, if most elusive, of dreams. Today the development of nuclear weapons has made peace imperative, while the continuing build-up of nuclear weaponry has made it evermore precarious.

The realities of global security have changed profoundly; yet our concept of security and our approach to achieving it is still deeply entrenched in our past attitudes and behaviour and the institutions devoted to perpetuating them. We must now make the transition to a new concept of security and to new approaches to achieving security on a global scale.

The basic changes in the military, economic, ecological and social conditions which drive this transition are only beginning to evoke the attention of political leaders. They are now beginning to talk about these issues, but this has not yet produced any significant movement towards the changes in international behaviour and the strengthening of the instruments and institutions of international cooperation which the transition requires.

The recent renewal of interest in multilateralism, particularly among the great powers is encouraging. But dealing effectively with the new realities of interdependence in which more and more issues of importance to nations are inter-related across sectoral and national boundaries requires more than a mere reversion to traditional multi-lateralism. The "new multilateralism" will clearly require strengthening the role and the capacity of multilateral agencies, notably the United Nations system. It is the only organization that is global in its scope, universal in its membership and mandated by the nations of the world through the United Nations Charter as the instrument for addressing the issues of world peace and security. The United Nations has also, through its initiatives and cooperative programs in the economic, social, environmental, humanitarian and human rights fields recognized and sought to address these important issues which bear on global and human security.

While the leadership of the great powers is indispensable to this process, it is not sufficient. The rest of the world, and particularly the developing world which comprises the majority of the world's people and nations, must become full partners in it. And the issues that concern them most and affect their interest must get special attention – issues such as eradication of poverty, hunger and disease and the development of the kind of viable, more equitable and growing economies which will enable them to meet the needs and aspirations of their people.

For many in the developing world, as Ambassador Roche points out, the risks to survival are acute and immediate – hunger, malnutrition and lack of access to the necessary ingredients of a decent life. They are caught up in a vicious circle in which the immediate economic imperatives of survival force them to undermine and destroy the ecological and natural resource systems on which their future depends. The report of the World Commission of Environment and Development makes clear the need to break this vicious circle by a transition to sustainable development through a synthesis of the ecological and economic dimensions of human activity. This in turn will require reduction in, and containment of, the conflicts within the Third World which are exacting intolerable economic and human costs they can so ill afford.

Nowhere have these issues been better or more clearly set out than in this very important book. Douglas Roche describes the background to the historic opportunity we now face with the intimate knowledge and authority of one who has had a long and deep interest in issues of development, disarmament and peace as analyst, as prophet, and as activist, most recently in his capacity as Canada's Ambassador for Disarmament. No one understands these issues better; no one explains them better and no one has worked more devotedly or effectively towards overcoming the attitudinal, policy and institutional inertia that has frustrated progress towards peace and security in the past. This lends special credibility to his analysis and the programme of practical measures he has proposed for the achievement of global security in the 1990's. And it makes equally credible his scenarios for the tragic consequences of our failure to rise to this historic opportunity.

Maurice Strong is President of the World Federation of United Nations Associations. A leading Canadian authority on global security issues, he was the first President of the Canadian International Development Agency and the first Executive Director of the United Nations Environment Programme. Mr. Strong served as Under-Secretary General of the United Nations. He was also a member of the World Commission on Environment and Development (Brundtland Report).

List of Acronyms

ABM	Anti-Ballistic Missile (Treaty) 1972
ALCM	Air-launched cruise missile
ACM	Advanced (stealth) cruise missile
CCACD	Canadian Centre for Arms Control and Disarmament
CIDA	Canadian International Development Agency
CIIPS	Canadian Institute for International Peace and Security
CPA	Canadian Peace Alliance
CPPNW	Canadian Physicians for the Prevention of Nuclear War
CFCs	Carboflourocarbons
CBM	Confidence-building measure
CD	Conference on Disarmament: 40 nations, Geneva
CFE	Conventional Forces in Europe: NATO and Warsaw Pact negotiations opened in Vienna, March, 1989
CSCE	Conference on Security and Co-operation in Europe: (35 countries including the U.S. and Canada)
CTB	Comprehensive test ban
CW	Chemical weapon
GLCM	Ground-launched cruise missile
FAO	Food and Agriculture Organization of the United Nations
IAEA	International Atomic Energy Agency
ICBM	Inter-continental ballistic missile
INF	Intermediate-range Nuclear Force (Treaty) 1987
MAD	Mutual assured destruction
MIRV	Multiple independently targetable re-entry vehicle
ODA	Official Development Assistance
NGO	Non-governmental organization
NPT	Non-proliferation Treaty (1968): largest multilateral arms control treaty in world, signed by 140 nations
NWFZ	Nuclear weapon-free zone
PGA	Parliamentarians Global Action
PNE	Peaceful Nuclear Explosions (Treaty)
PTB	Partial Test Ban (Treaty)
SALT	Strategic arms limitation talks
SIPRI	Stockholm International Peace Research Institute
SDI	Strategic Defence Initiative
SLBM	Submarine-launched ballistic missile
SLCM	Sea-launched cruise missile
SNF	Short-range nuclear forces
START	Strategic arms reduction talks
TTBT	Threshold Test-Ban Treaty
UNCTAD	United Nations Conference on Trade and Development
UNDC	United Nations Disarmament Commission

Introduction:

Two Futures and a Critical Choice

July 22, 2009. At 6:00 a.m. radio station WCBS in New York City received a phone call stating an important letter could be found in a flower pot two blocks away. A reporter was dispatched and brought back a typed note threatening to blow up Manhattan in 36 hours unless the United States government delivered $1 billion to a numbered bank account in Geneva. The note was signed "International Syndicate," a multinational band of terrorists from Syria, Libya, Nigeria, Brazil and India that had recently united to obtain, as the Central Intelligence Agency report put it, "retribution for the alleged wrongs committed by the major powers on the suffering people of the world." WCBS immediately sent the letter to the Federal Bureau of Investigation and, following a policy adopted by the media not to panic the population, sat on the story. Nuclear threats had been received before; all had proven groundless.

Nevertheless, the editors in the newsroom were uneasy. The summer of 2009 was unlike any previous time. The anger of huge numbers of young people throughout Asia, Africa and Latin America no longer seemed containable. Economic breakdown in many developing countries was now spreading, the effect of the countries of the South no longer able to cope with the elementary task of feeding their own people. The world had become a place where ten percent of the population lived in high-technology and wealthy countries controlling three quarters of the world's wealth while the other 90 percent where jammed into oppressive areas with access to only a quarter of the world's wealth. The situation worsened every day, with the South absorbing 90 percent of the growth in global population which had now passed eight billion.

Debt and militarism siphoned off the efforts of the developing regions, while the developed countries stagnated from deficits exacerbated by military spending. The swollen conglomerations of two dozen megacities (Mexico City now had the same population as Canada), unable to provide even enough drinking water, spawned crime and terrorism. Hungry, hopeless, embittered and desperate,

11

the young began rioting on three continents. Commerce was shut down, tourist hotels blown up. The major powers flew in troops to quell the rioters. The International Atomic Energy Agency reported that terrorists had acquired sufficient materials for "backpack" nuclear bombs.

Claiming that the major powers had no intention of eliminating their nuclear weapons, 15 countries (Syria, Israel, Iran, Libya among them) had, even before the 21st century began, developed primitive nuclear bombs to increase their political power and stature in world councils. The Non-Proliferation Treaty, designed to halt the proliferation of nuclear weapons, broke down in 1995. The spread of nuclear weapons raised temperatures in regional conflicts to a constant boiling point.

The third generation of nuclear weapons, invulnerable, faster and more precise than ever before, was deployed by the superpowers who, while talking peace among themselves, were now spending most of their time and energy trying to calm down raging regional uprisings. Local wars (the 33 of the 1980's grew to 45 by 2000) were using munitions so rapidly, particularly missiles, that arms merchants in the big developing countries built their own consortiums to supplement the arms bought from the major powers. The U.N. Secretary-General continued to send his emissaries around the world, but combatants had long since stopped listening.

The costs of the global arms race shot past the $2 trillion level, siphoning off more and more human and physical resources. The decades-long diversion of scientific and engineering talent from productive civilian technological development to military research was now crippling economic growth in both the North and the South. Moreover, the destruction of tropical forests, diminishing the habitat of thousands of species, the extension of deserts caused by over-grazing and brush clearance, the oil spills, industrial wastes and sewage aggravation were so polluting water and air that acid rain, drought and flooding were all playing havoc with the ordinary processes of life. Warming of the climate eroded coastlines and devastated low-lying countries. Ecological refugees mounted into the millions.

The world chaos culminated with the extortion letter from the International Syndicate. The letter was proven authentic, but the U.S. government refused to give in. The hours ticked by; the extortionists made two phone calls to the White House. Crisis teams were assembled. Every suspected terrorist on the Eastern seaboard was picked up by police. The experts believed that, in the end, the threat would prove to be a hoax.

But one minute after the 36-hour deadline, a searing flash ripped through West 14th Street in the southern part of Manhattan. Within five seconds, as a mushroom cloud started to form overhead, every building in a 20-block radius collapsed. Fires raged out of control. The windows in the United Nations Secretariat, two miles away, shattered. The electricity and water supplies and traffic were paralyzed. The public feared more bombs would explode and the panic lasted for three days. No one could be sure of the death toll, but at least 175,000 were killed outright. It took a month to fly the 90,000 wounded to the few medical centres around North America and Europe equipped to deal with burn victims. Most of them, however, died.

For the first time, the United Nations held an emergency meeting of the Security Council at the summit level.

SCENARIO NO. 2

July 22, 2009. At 11:00 a.m. the annual summit meeting of the United Nations Security Council opened. The heads of government of the original five permanent members, the United States, Soviet Union, United Kingdom, France and China were present along with the heads of four more states, India, Japan, Nigeria and Brazil, admitted to permanent membership in 1995. The ten non-permanent members were also present. The first item on the agenda was approval of the world 2010 Global Action Plan.

The 2010 Plan was the final stage in a process of world reform that started in 1995, the 50th anniversary of the founding of the U.N. Although a world war had been averted for half a century, the cumulative crises of regional wars (Vietnam, Iran-Iraq, Afghanistan, Angola), the global arms race, world poverty, environmental destruction and violations of human rights had finally shocked governments everywhere into action. The fear of economic and social catastrophe galvanized a handful of political leaders backed by a new international coalition of leading non-governmental organizations into pressing for a world conference on security. The momentum of the U.N.'s 50th anniversary provided the spark for the proposal, the media everywhere suddenly discovered its possible significance, and the conference was called under the chairmanship of the Secretary-General of the United Nations, the only person the major powers would trust.

Attended by every country in the world, the conference was entrusted with hammering out a world security system.

The conference lasted nearly a decade. Just agreeing on how problems of a military, social, economic, humanitarian and ecological nature threaten the security of countries and individuals took three years. But gradually the idea that special agencies to manage transborder problems were necessary to ensure global peace took hold. A World Disarmament Agency, a World Peace-Keeping Agency, a World Verification Agency, a World Development Agency and a World Environmental Agency were all proposed with the power to effect regulations passed by the Security Council.

At first, the resistance of the major powers to encroachment on their national sovereignty was enormous. But, pushed by powerful waves of public opinion, they eventually conceded that their own interests in world stability required new forms of planetary management. The world-wide and imaginative celebration of the year 2000, when people began to focus on how decent and secure life everywhere could be, generated new currents of support for change. The enlargement of the Security Council, to make it more representative of the major regions of the world, complemented the 1992 economic union of Europe and gave added impetus to a new process of international cooperation.

Even before the Security Conference ended, beneficial results of the enlarged search for security began to be noted. The superpowers opened discussions to reduce their strategic nuclear weapons to a minimal level of deterrence, a multilateral agreement to reduce conventional forces in Europe to a purely defensive posture was reached, a universal ban on the production of chemical weapons was implemented, debt reduction plans for the developing countries were started in ways that did not shut off their capacity for growth, the industrial countries all agreed to move immediately to a new international aid target of one percent of gross national product, development programmes harmonized with environmental needs were begun.

With expanded governmental thinking sustained by public opinion and a widening process of education about global security, the world climate had improved sufficiently by 2005 to enable the Security Council to begin organizing the new world agencies recommended by the Security Conference. The new agencies would have the authority to oversee the process of general and complete disarmament down to the level required for internal security (which had originally been agreed to at the 1978 U.N. Special Session on Disarmament); verify the process with standing international teams of inspectors; maintain a permanent U.N. Police Force to separate parties in a conflict; cut down the arms trade between nations; ensure that international financial and trade regulations would not discriminate against developing countries; develop a mechanism for the transfer of funds released by declining military expenditures to greater world productivity.

The assessment of these new approaches to global security and approval of the 2010 Plan for full implementation over the next decade was the work of the July 22, 2009 Security Council meeting. There was by no means total harmony. In the private session, prior to going before the cameras in the public chamber, voices were raised and the table pounded. At one stage the Secretary-General had to intervene with the warning that global security was indeed costly – in terms of giving up some of the old and cherished ideas of national sovereignty as well as the financial cost of an enlarged United Nations system. "If you want to walk out the door back to the chaos when no one anywhere could be secure, go ahead," he challenged the rebellious faction. For a moment, the room was still. Then the Secretary-General said, the hint of a smile on his face, "Let's go before the cameras."

Establishing the structures to avert global chaos and move the world to a higher level of creativity is now a matter of global survival. The 1990's have the potential to become the decade in which humankind moves the world towards a new form of global security, a world in which countries cooperate in efforts to reduce the risk of war, limit arms, accelerate development, protect the environment. These moves would prepare the way for the abolition of nuclear weapons. A worldwide coalition of forces, involving people-to-people movements as well as governments, is necessary to bring this about. It requires a modern effort paralleling the struggle to eliminate slavery and colonialism. This is undoubtedly a long, tortuous, process. Vision is needed, the kind of vision that Canada has shown before in its peacekeeping leadership. In the crucial decade of the 1990's, stronger Canadian involvement in global security issues could produce a reblossoming of Canada's multilateral approach to the world that has not been seen since the 1950's.

First, we have to deal with the contradictions of our time. The decade of the 1980's drew to a close on a roller coaster of emotion.

Contradiction was the dominant theme. The persistent peace initiatives of Soviet leader Mikhail Gorbachev, who proved as popular as a rock star during a visit to West Germany, caught the imagination of people everywhere who dared to dream that the long Cold War between East and West might finally be over. Suddenly, a cold chill permeated the air as the hard-line Communist government of China sent in its tanks to massacre student protesters in Beijing's Tiananmen Square. In Poland, however, the formation of the first non-Communist government in 40 years provided stunning evidence that the world is witnessing the breakup of the postwar order in Eastern Europe.

Despite an "outbreak of peace," nations still prepare for war. The United States and the Soviet Union concluded a treaty to eliminate ground-launched intermediate and shorter-range nuclear weapons, but their deployment of sea-launched cruise missiles will more than compensate for this loss. The arms race, in its nuclear and conventional dimensions, roars on. More than 50 nuclear warheads and nine nuclear reactors are scattered on the ocean floors, the result of accidents involving American and Soviet ships, bombers and rockets.

The world is spending one-third more on arms of all kinds than on the health care of all 5.2 billion people on earth. That number will likely rise to 8.5 billion by 2025, when most of humanity will live in developing countries unable to meet the basic human needs of current populations. The advances in medicine, agriculture, energy production, electronics, cybernetics and laser technology are lifting civilization to new heights, but in the last half of the 1980's, in the 37 poorest countries, spending per head on health has been reduced by 50 percent and on education by 25 percent. In Southern Africa, more children have died in the Angola and Mozambique conflicts than the total number of people killed in the Hiroshima and Nagasaki nuclear blasts. Food riots have broken out in Latin American and African countries where economic breakdown is rampant. The world illiteracy rate is rising and the number of illiterate adults will be close to one billion by the year 2000.

Growing global problems are beyond any one nation's capacity to solve: the number of refugees, 14.5 million, has never been higher; the AIDS epidemic is now felt in 146 countries; international terrorism took a record 658 lives in 1988.

Though humanity's welfare remains tightly linked to the land, 35 percent of the earth's land surface is threatened by desertification; global climatic patterns are being disrupted, wreaking havoc on food production and community life around the globe for generations to come. The greed that drives the destruction of forests has come to its pinnacle in Peru. Driven by American and European demand for cocaine, Peruvian coca growers have chopped down huge stretches of precious Amazon rain forest to expand plantations and sow drug crops. They are also dumping millions of gallons of toxic chemicals into highlands and headwaters. Environmental damage is not some "far-away" problem. Canadians have turned the St. Lawrence River into a sewage system where toxic chemicals are wiping out beluga whales. And carbon dioxide emissions are 16 times worse in Canada than in the developing world.

The contradictions and gross discordancies of the modern world abound. It is anachronistic to the point of absurdity to have two blocs of highly developed nations devoting such enormous resources to armaments while so much is to be done to improve the human condition. It is a scenario more suitable to the religious wars of the European middle ages than to the space age. We celebrate the good news of small victories and overlook the trend lines of worsening problems that jeopardize the planet as a whole. The pile-up of weapons, nuclear and conventional, the imbalances in populations, wealth, food and health services, the degradation of the environment – all these problems are now interlocking. None can be solved alone by any one government. The security of nations and individuals must now be addressed in its wholeness. The threads of societal values, cultures, the political process, and public policy in domestic and international affairs must be woven together into a coherent management system for the planet.

A comprehensive approach to global security would produce a system of world governance, with the United Nation as the key element. This would not be a supra-national world government. Rather, nations would agree to implement the U.N.'s global strategies for disarmament, development and the environment and put in place the structures for world law.

This movement of history, for it has already begun, is what this book is about. I write with a sense of urgency, knowing that the global problems are worsening faster than the application of piece-meal solutions, and yet with a sense of patience, appreciating how long it takes to change human habits. The record speaks for itself. I have been working on these problems for 12 years as a Member of Parliament and five years as Canada's Ambassador for Disarmament. In that 17-year period, beginning in 1972, every one of the world's major security, economic and social problems has worsened. In 1972, 400 million people were malnourished; today there are 770 million. In 1972, there were 22,000 nuclear weapons in existence, today there are 52,000. In 1972, the world spent $534 billion on arms; today the figure is $1 trillion.

The most searing fact that I have learned in 17 years in active politics and United Nations diplomacy is the huge gap that exists between the minimum expectations of people who think deeply about world conditions and the maximum that governments achieve. The very best that governments are doing today is to manage crises; they are not rooting out the core of the crises. They are putting band-aids on a cancerous condition. Too many politicians, diplomats and bureaucrats of the Western countries carry on with the old assumptions that the world is a place of confrontation and our side has to stay on top. The world is being transformed before our eyes – a new human community is struggling to be born – but the government processes go on with business as usual. The attitude that the West is superior and automatically deserves to be in control of the resources and wealth of the world produces a continuing complacency and smugness which are delusionary and dangerous.

The most perilous of all assumptions is the belief that the Western strategy of nuclear deterrence is essential to our security. Maintaining nuclear deterrence into the 21st century is what will lead to our downfall. It is a central argument of this book that nuclear deterrence is not an aid to peace, it is an impediment to peace. It prevents genuine nuclear disarmament. It maintains an unacceptable hegemony over non-nuclear nations. It fuels the arms race around the world. It spawns a militarism that is choking off development for the poorest half of the world's population. It is a fundamental obstacle to achieving a new age of global security.

I write as an abolitionist. I want the world rid of nuclear weapons. However, the political structures are still dominated by those who think that nuclear weapons are the price of peace. The nuclear technocrats continue their charade of Western vulnerability in order to get the appropriations for new nuclear weapons. They get away with it because politicians, whether they believe in the need for more arms or not, are afraid of being perceived as weak. Governments are for disarmament, but they will not take the steps necessary to stop the arms race.

I worked inside the system to try to change it. Just as I always felt it an honour to be able to speak and vote in Parliament on behalf of my constituents, I always felt it a privilege to represent Canada in disarmament meetings at the United Nations. I rejoiced when I found others who felt as I did. At the U.N., one of the strongest advocates of genuine disarmament was Richard Butler, Australia's Ambassador for Disarmament, who regularly brought to the Barton Group challenging views about the need for Western movement to respond to the unprecedented opportunity provided by Soviet leader Gorbachev. The Barton Group (named after former Canadian Ambassador William Barton) is composed of the 16 NATO countries plus Australia, New Zealand, Japan and Ireland and is chaired by the Canadian Ambassador for Disarmament. It meets regularly at the Canadian Mission to the U.N. to discuss Western disarmament positions.

At one of my first meetings in 1984, I ended by noting the need for better resolutions to end the arms race. At the conclusion, the U.S. ambassador privately remonstrated with me that "the U.S. is not engaged in an arms race." He reported this exchange to officials in Washington who immediately lodged a complaint against me with the Canadian government. Two months later, when I said on CTV's *Question Period* that the West should consider a "selective freeze" on the development of new weapons, the U.S. government again complained to Ottawa of my "unhelpful" approach. Another time, U.S. officials derided my pre-ambassadorial role as International Chairman of Parliamentarians Global Action, which launched in 1984 the Six-Nation Initiative to press both superpowers to resume nuclear weapons negotiations.

I was not the U.S. government's favourite foreign ambassador (even though at one stage of my life I lived nine years in the United States and three of my children were born there). But my problems were small compared to some of the stormy encounters in the history of our two countries. In his memoirs, Lester B. Pearson describes the dressing down he received from Lyndon Johnson for criticizing U.S. bombing in Vietnam. "The problem of Canada-United States relations is always with us," Pearson observed. Shortly after being appointed Ambassador, I visited Howard Green (who died in 1989), Canada's External Affairs Minister from 1959 to 1963. Green is remembered at the U.N. to this day as a staunch advocate of disarmament. For two hours, he told me in detail the kinds of problems I would encounter, and he ended with this statement, which was both a warning and a prediction: "Just remember, your biggest problems will be with the Americans and the Canadian bureaucracy." Green was right on both counts. The two problems are inter-connected, as I explain more fully in Chapter 6. For example, I was never able to convince the bureaucracy to have Canada vote "yes" on nuclear freeze resolutions at the United Nations, because the U.S. is so firmly opposed. If the U.S. ever changed its mind, Canada would quickly support a freeze.

During the 106 meetings of the Barton Group that I chaired, I had to steer it carefully between Ireland and Greece, which were ready for complete disarmament, and the U.S. and U.K., which definitely were not. At one stage, Ireland threatened to leave the group in protest against the heavy-handed tactics of the Americans. But I prevailed on the Irish to stay because we needed their views.

The Canadian government stood behind me, otherwise I would not have been allowed to remain in the sensitive position of Chairman of the Western countries. In 1988, Canada proposed me as a candidate for the chairmanship of the United Nations Political and Security (First) Committee, which rotates each year, and I was elected unanimously. To prepare, I journeyed around the world, consulting with governments in every region. The chairmanship was a highlight for me because, using the contacts I had built up over the years, I was able to move the committee towards more consensus resolutions and mergers. In fact, the committee passed 40.8 percent of its resolutions by consensus, the highest percentage ever. Yet on the key nuclear issues, the divisions remained as wide as ever.

When the First Committee chairmanship was over, I decided that I had done as much within the Canadian system as I could and that I wanted to spend the remainder of my life speaking out frankly to help inform the public about the urgent need to stop the arms race, eliminate de-humanizing poverty and save the environment before the multiple world crises explode around us. I especially want to help train the future leaders of the 21st century.

In the years I have spent on the disarmament issue, no experience has so moved me as visiting Hiroshima. I wrote in my journal:

> As I walked through the museum, looking at the terrible scenes of such massive pain, I fell into contemplation, unsure whether I wanted to be silent or rage at the violations of humanity. Did I want to study it more or reject it as too much for the human mind to take in? I wrote in the guest book: "In silence, in memory, in hope." I listened to the A-bomb survivors tell their ghastly stories, wondering why they were in Hiroshima in 1945 and I was in Ottawa, and felt a new solidarity with them. I knew in my heart that I must work against nuclear weapons, not accept them as the guarantors of peace. . . Every arms negotiator should be compelled to visit Hiroshima before sitting down to discuss the abstractions of throw-weights and re-entry systems.

My experience at international disarmament forums in Geneva and Vienna as well as New York has convinced me that significant disarmament will not occur while governments are still swayed by the outmoded idea that security is equated with weaponry. An attitudinal change, in politicians, negotiators and the public, is required to build the conditions for true human security. As well as disarmament, global security requires international cooperation for development and environmental protection. None of this will be attained without a massive outpouring of public concern, driving the political processes into the new age.

I retain a sense of optimism that this consciousness-raising and political action can be achieved. We have more knowledge than ever before about how the planet works. The tools of technology are available. That knowledge and those tools were not available 75 years ago when World War I broke out or 50 years ago when World War II started. A common vision for global security must be acquired to make sure that the second July 22, 2009 scenario, not the first, is received by our children and grandchildren as their legacy from us. We must seize the present moment.

PART ONE:

Of Chaos and Creativity

Chapter One

The 1980's:
How the Arms Race Produced World Crises

On December 12, 1984, as the United Nations' First Committee, which deals with disarmament matters, was reporting to the General Assembly, U.N. Secretary-General Javier Perez de Cuellar took the unusual step of coming to the podium.

Six years earlier at the First U.N. Special Session on Disarmament, the nations of the world had adopted by consensus a Final Document containing a Programme of Action for general and complete disarmament. Now the world picture had turned bleak. A second U.N. Special Session on Disarmament in 1982 ended in failure. The United States and its Western allies had begun deploying cruise and Pershing missiles in Europe. The Soviet Union pressed ahead with its arms buildup and walked out of bilateral negotiations with the U.S. The 40-nation Conference on Disarmament in Geneva was virtually paralyzed. Conventional arms negotiations between NATO and the Warsaw Pact in Vienna were at a standstill. All during the fall of 1984 at the U.N., the Soviets and Americans traded invective. "The United States is preparing for a first nuclear strike," declared the Soviet delegate. "We cannot but wonder whether the [Soviet] walkout may be the forerunner of a breakout from agreed restraints and restrictions," answered the U.S. representative.

In this gloomy setting, Perez de Cuellar sent word that he would make an extraordinary intervention. It was a speech that had been building up. In 1982, giving his first annual report, he excoriated the nuclear and conventional arms buildup, contrasting it to world poverty of vast proportions – "a deprivation inexplicable in terms either of available resources or the money and ingenuity spent on armaments and war." He criticized governments for ignoring their own signatures on the U.N. Charter. "We are perilously near to a new international anarchy."

A Peruvian diplomat, Javier Perez de Cuellar is a soft-spoken man, rather courtly in manner, almost reluctant to be the world leader his office demands. But by 1984, the state of the world clearly alarmed him. A nuclear war could lead to the extinction of humanity, he warned, and then pointed to the two superpowers: "By what right do they decide the fate of all humanity?"

From Scandinavia to Latin America, from Europe and Africa to the Far East, the destiny of every man, woman and child is affected by the actions of the United States and the Soviet Union. In a conflict of only hours or minutes, the entire work of civilization could be obliterated. "There can be no greater arrogance." The Secretary-General went on to demolish the argument that nuclear weapons and the strategy of deterrence have kept the peace. "If nuclear weapons are indeed peace-keepers, does it follow that they ought to be acquired by every nation on earth? On the contrary, it is clear that to rely on nuclear deterrence is to accept a perpetual community of fear." Moreover, it is unreasonable to expect other nations not to obtain nuclear weapons while the superpowers indulge in uncontrolled expansion of theirs. "I appeal for a renewed effort towards a comprehensive test ban treaty. No single multilateral agreement could have a greater effect on limiting the further refinement of nuclear weapons. A comprehensive test ban treaty is the litmus test of the real willingness to pursue nuclear disarmament." Rather than stopping the endless arms race, disarmament discussions have taken on a life of their own. "All too often it seems as if the players are only moving their lethal powers in a global chess game."

At a time of uncertainty for the young and despair for the poor and the hungry, Perez de Cuellar added, "we have truly mortgaged our future to the arms race – both nuclear and conventional." The arms trade is like the drug trade: both kill or seriously harm the receiver and debase the supplier. The link between disarmament and development must be elaborated. Concrete and far-sighted preparation for the conversion of industries from military to civilian production are needed. "In the nuclear age, decisions affecting war and peace cannot be left to military strategists or even to governments. They are indeed the responsibility of every man and woman. It is the responsibility of all of us in this chamber to break the cycle of mistrust and insecurity and respond to humanity's yearning for peace."

It was the strongest speech that Perez de Cuellar has given to date in his two terms as U.N. Secretary-General. It contributed to the world pressure building up on the superpowers.

Nuclear arms negotiations resumed between the United States and the Soviet Union in 1985, leading to the Intermediate Nuclear Forces Treaty (INF), eliminating two categories of nuclear weapons in Europe: those with ranges between 1,000 and 5,500 kilometres and those with ranges between 500 and 1,000 kilometres. The INF Treaty, celabrated with television pictures of Presidents Reagan and Gorbachev cuddling children in Red Square in Moscow, was hailed as a disarmament breakthrough. It was a breakthrough because it was the first treaty to establish reductions rather than put a ceiling on growth. In 1988, the first year of its implementation, 700 such missiles on both sides were destroyed. For the first time ever, Soviet and American verification teams have been stationed in each other's countries.

Yet the INF represented a cut of only four percent of all nuclear weapons. Even this minor reduction is offset as the military move to compensate for the loss of INF weapons with other types of weapon systems. Furthermore, NATO, in particular the U.S. and the U.K., has been anxious to modernize its short-range nuclear systems rather than negotiate their elimination.

The INF Treaty is an important achievement. However it has merely scratched the surface of disarmament. The real test lies in U.S.-USSR negotiations aimed at cutting long-range nuclear arms (START). The joint draft text currently under discussion sets an upper limit of 1,600 launchers and a ceiling of 6,000 warheads for each side. No more than 4,900 of the 6,000 can be warheads carried by ballistic missiles, the remaining 1,100 consisting of cruise missiles and bombs. Under this arrangement, reductions will not be 50 percent, as publicly projected, but closer to 30 percent, leaving the two sides with as many strategic nuclear weapons as they had when Perez de Cuellar warned of anarchy in the world.

Most worrying of all is the lack of limits on sea-launched cruise missiles (SLCMs). This question has been battled back and forth by the two sides. The Soviet Union has offered low ceilings on conventional and nuclear SLCMs, but the U.S. is hesitant to discuss the question because of the difficulties involved in verifying SLCM limits and the strategic importance the U.S. attaches to the missiles. In the absence of limits, SLCMs will nullify the numerical reductions made in START.

Most importantly, modernization remains uncontrolled. All five nuclear nations (U.S., USSR, U.K., France, China) are pushing ahead with modernization. New long-range bomber aircraft were introduced in the U.S. and Soviet forces in 1988. After years of secrecy, the U.S. B-2 stealth bomber was unveiled; 132 of these supersonic aircraft will cost $68.8 billion. The Soviet Blackjack A supersonic bomber was declared operational after a decade of development. The most powerful weapons coming on stream in the U.S. (the Trident II D-5 Submarine-launched ballistic missile and the advanced cruise missile, for example) will not be prohibited. Nor will the equivalent weapon systems on the Soviet side. As a result, both sides are making their nuclear arsenals more efficient. Older weapons will be retired and replaced with newer, faster and more accurate weapons. Under the guise of modernization, the arms race hurtles ahead. And it is all being done in the name of deterrence.

Over many years of debate about the possibility of limiting nuclear war and defending against nuclear weapons, deterrence has remained the central tenet of thinking about nuclear weapons. Nuclear deterrence is based on mutual vulnerability. Deterrence is said to work when both sides have the ability to inflict unacceptable damage on the attacker even after having being subjected to a nuclear attack. Crucial to this idea is the assumption that neither side has the capability of launching a first strike which could completely eliminate the other's ability to retaliate. Unable to attack with impunity, the attacker is thus deterred from initiating hostilities by the knowledge that any attack would be suicidal. This relationship is referred to as mutual assured destruction or MAD.

In 1963, U.S. Secretary of Defence Robert McNamara determined that a minimum level of survivable forces could guarantee second-strike capability. That is, with all factors taken into consideration, a certain level of forces could provide an assured ability to inflict unacceptable damage after an attack. Forces above this level were justified as needed for damage limitation – reducing the destructive capabilities of an incoming attack. The need to improve "damage limitation" and "strengthen" deterrence are reasons that have been used to justify a continued, virtually unchecked, build-up and modernization of nuclear forces. In spite of McNamara's conclusion that a minimum level of assured destruction capability could be determined, both sides have continued to participate in an arms race where the quantity and quality of weapons have continually increased. Although force levels are so high that numbers matter little to the maintenance of deterrence, the need not to be perceived as lagging behind the other plays a major role in the deterrence game.

Those who argue in favour of deterrence maintain that deterrence has "kept the peace" since 1945 by preventing war between the superpowers. In spite of other conflicts that have occurred around the world since 1945, the lack of direct U.S.-Soviet conflict and especially the absence of conflict in Europe are seen as important achievements. It is also argued that as long as nuclear weapons continue to exist, nuclear deterrence, as the strategy for managing the situation, must be maintained, since the most convincing way to ensure that nuclear weapons will not be used is to threaten the potential user with the very same destruction.

Essentially, the West has supported nuclear deterrence as the only way to guarantee that the Soviets will not invade the West. There has been a persistent fear that Western values of freedom and abundance are threatened by a perception of Soviet expansionism and world dominance. Defenders of deterrence hold that the West, protecting a way of life that is built on liberty, has an obligation to oppose Soviet power, and needs the nuclear deterrent to do so. The Soviets must know that they will be obliterated if they launch a nuclear attack; and they must know that if they endeavour to overrun Western nations with their superior conventional forces in Europe, the West will respond with nuclear weapons. In this light, the Soviets are the enemy. This is the commonly accepted moral justification in the West for threatening to use nuclear weapons. The horror of nuclear holocaust, in the event that deterrence breaks down, is judged in the political order to be a lesser harm. In short, the risks of nuclear destruction that accompany a policy of nuclear deterrence are deemed more acceptable than the risks of developing a diplomatic and political alternative to dealing with the Soviets.

Only lately, as the public has begun to rebel against the incessant demands of nuclear accountancy, has it become better understood that deterrence is a flawed policy. Not only does it commit us to threaten the use of a weapon we know can never be used because to do so would be to invite our own destruction but it also forces us to build even more sophisticated systems. We go on stockpiling nuclear weapons far beyond the original needs of deterrence in the now certain knowledge that all human life is at stake given an error, terrorist action, or a government's designed first strike. With the vertical and horizontal multiplication of nuclear weapons now playing such a critical role in international relations, the potential breakdown of the deterrence system is greatly increased. The nuclear powers' willingness to sustain deterrence has created a situation in which other states want to join in the game but without any guarantees that they will play by the rules established by the original nuclear powers.

A prerequisite for sustaining public support for nuclear deterrence is the image of the Soviet threat. That threat has always been exaggerated. Now that the image of the threat is receding in the Western mind as a result of the initiatives taken by Gorbachev – now that the Cold War is ending as the Soviets open a new chapter in their history and are trying to build a constructive relationship with the West – it is imperative for the West to reassess its reliance on nuclear deterrence as an essential strategy for security. There are powerful elements in the political, bureaucratic and media establishments that will not countenance any challenging of the core strategy of Western protection. But nuclear deterrence must be challenged by a hard-headed and very realistic assessment of the opportunity afforded the world by the end of the Cold War. Not to do so is to fall back into a state of pessimism about the human condition that will almost inevitably lead to the use of nuclear weapons.

The notion that only military targets would be destroyed in a nuclear exchange is an illusion. For deterrence to work, a credible threat must be created to destroy a country's war-fighting ability, including its industrial and economic base. Urban populations would be directly attacked even if a nuclear exchange could be limited to selective targets. Deterrence, then, is a direct threat to kill non-combatants.

The smallest of the strategic nuclear weapons deployed by both superpowers is several times as powerful as the bomb used against Hiroshima in 1945 which produced 130,000 immediate casualties and razed 90 percent of the city; most are ten or twenty times as powerful. In less than 30 minutes, a single MX missile, or its Soviet counterpart, can deliver a destructive force equivalent to more than 200 Hiroshima bombs to within 90 metres of a target 11,000 kilometres away. In 1979, U.S. President Jimmy Carter said, "Just one of our relatively invulnerable Poseidon submarines carries enough warheads to destroy every large and medium-size city in the Soviet Union." But one such submarine, it seems, is not enough. The U.S. has 24 Poseidons and is replacing these with the even more powerful Trident. It is estimated that the land, sea and air-based arsenals of strategic weapons possessed by both the United States and the Soviet Union could destroy the world 14 times over.

Leading physicians have warned that even a limited nuclear exchange would cause death and injury to people on a scale unprecedented in human history and would present any remaining medical services with insoluble problems. People not immediately burned to death, blown apart or asphyxiated would find themselves in a nightmare world populated by the dead, dying and insane. Food, crops and land would be contaminated, water undrinkable. Moreover, as a United Nations study on "nuclear winter" shows, the indirect effects could kill billions through the breakdown of communications, transportation and financial systems and all of this compounded by temperature decrease, suppressed monsoons, and increased ultraviolet radiation.

In the name of deterrence, the arms race has been fueled by new technologies that have made nuclear weapons more powerful, more flexible, and shortened the time interval from launch to impact to only minutes. One side or the other is always marginally ahead in testing and deployment, so the other side catches up. Since 1945, the lead in the race for improved systems has switched back and forth between the superpowers. The U.S. led with the atom bomb, intercontinental bomber, and thermonuclear bomb. The USSR caught up and plunged ahead with the intercontinental ballistic missile (ICBM) and man-made satellite. The U.S. took the lead with the submarine-launched ballistic missile and multiple warhead. The USSR countered with the anti-ballistic missile and caught up to the U.S. advance in multiple independently-targeted re-entry vehicle (MIRV). The U.S. went ahead again with the long-range cruise missile and neutron bomb. Between 1982 and 1988, the U.S. and the Soviet Union increased the number of strategic nuclear weapons in their arsenals by more than one-third, the U.S. reaching a total of 14,600, the Soviets 11,700. New systems of mobile launchers are now being developed by both sides. Both have engaged in research programmes for a strategic defence system, with the Reagan administration giving top priority to its Strategic Defence Initiative (SDI) programme, which promised a technologically unobtainable nuclear shield.

A discussion of deterrence centers on the U.S. and Soviet Union because they possess about 97 percent of the estimated 52,000 nuclear weapons in the world. Although there are always variations in specific categories, an approximate strategic parity exists between the two superpowers. The remainder are in the hands of France with about 450 warheads, the U.K. with 300 and China with 350. These three "lesser" states also have active plans to modernize further their nuclear forces over the next decade. The official nuclear "club" of five happens to be the same five which hold permanent seats on the U.N. Security Council, the most powerful legal and political instrument in the international community.

The number of nuclear weapons states is, however, growing. Six additional countries – Argentina, Brazil, India, Israel, Pakistan and South Africa – are believed to have nuclear weapons or to be on the threshold of such capabilities. Moreover, the Stockholm International Peace Research Institute (SIPRI) has identified 24 countries, most in the Third World, that either have ballistic missiles or are developing long-range rockets which can be used as ballistic missiles. Such missiles can be armed with chemical or nuclear warheads. In addition to the six having nuclear weapons' capability, these countries are: Afghanistan, Algeria, Cuba, Egypt, Greece, Indonesia, Iran, Iraq, North Korea, South Korea, Kuwait, Libya, Saudi Arabia, Syria, Taiwan, Turkey, North Yemen and South Yemen. All missile proliferation relies on foreign technology, whether for technical know-how or for inspiration, and countries with missile programmes are searching for accommodating suppliers, especially China and the Soviet Union, as well as pooling missile technology among themselves. The international response to missile proliferation in the Third World indicates no clear sense of direction. Some nations try to restrict transfers of missile technology; other governments license missile exports. The outlook for international control is poor.

The 1968 Non-Proliferation Treaty (NPT), signed by 140 nations, is designed to stop the horizontal spread of nuclear weapons. It has had some important success in transferring nuclear technology for peaceful purposes to developing countries while preventing the spread of weapons. But a number of important countries have not joined the NPT, and the Treaty itself is becoming weaker, since the major nuclear weapons parties to the NPT, the U.S., USSR and U.K., are not seen to be fulfilling their obligations to cease the arms race.

An end to testing is the first requisite to ceasing the arms race. In the years 1945- 87, the five nuclear states tested 1,669 times and India tested once (the U.S. 829 times, USSR 620, France 148, U.K. 41, China 30). Though the Soviets instituted a unilateral moratorium on testing in 1985, the U.S., which maintains testing for modernization purposes and to advance the SDI programme, would not join in. After 18 months, the Soviets resumed testing. In 1988, the year hailed as a breakthrough in East-West relations, the USSR tested 17 times, the U.S. 14, France 8, and China 1. It is claimed to be progress when the U.S. and USSR cooperate in monitoring each other's tests.

With the possession of nuclear weapons equated to power in the world, it is no wonder that more nations want into the "club." The nuclear powers themselves have clearly shown that they believe modernized nuclear weapons have great military and political value. While the management of Washington-Moscow relations has clearly improved (both leaders affirming that a nuclear war can never be won and must never be fought), the danger to the world continues through an accident, a terrorist action, or a planned strike in some regional conflict. The key to reducing the global arms race in both nuclear and conventional weapons is for both superpowers to come down from their nuclear mountain. Only then will it be possible for multilateral negotiations to reduce armaments everywhere.

Current multilateral efforts are weak and in many areas stalemated, as the U.N. Third Special Session on Disarmament in 1988 revealed in the failure to reach a consensus final statement. Although the Third Special Session ended in disarray, there was sufficient momentum generated to establish some important common ground, or as the U.N. Secretary-General put it, "a shared acceptance of some important propositions":

- Disarmament is not the exclusive responsibility of the two most powerful states but a joint undertaking of all states;
- While nuclear disarmament must continue to be the primary concern, conventional disarmament has acquired a new urgency;
- The qualitative aspect of the arms race needs to be addressed along with its quantitative aspect.
- National security needs to be viewed in the broader context of global issues and international concerns;
- Disarmament should be pursued along with efforts to resolve conflicts, build confidence and promote economic and social development.

But this step forward has been accompanied by a step back. The leading Western nations have backed away from their 1978 agreement on the Final Document of the First Special Session on Disarmament and blocked the passage of a moderately-worded Declaration of the 1990's as the Third Disarmament Decade, which was debated at the 1989 session of the United Nations Disarmament Commission.

However, the prospects are better now than at any time in the past for the successful conclusion a world-wide treaty banning the production of chemical weapons. And the outlook for conventional force reductions in Europe is better than it has ever been. The 35 nations of the Conference on Security and Cooperation in Europe (Europe plus the United States and Canada) did come to an agreement on the Stockholm Document of 1986, which establishes the right of East and West to monitor the other's troop maneuvers in Europe. This was an important step in building confidence that there would be no surprise attacks, but it was not disarmament. Opponents of serious arms reduction continue to argue that a conventional presence and short-range nuclear weapons are needed to reinforce Western strength in Europe.

THE ECONOMIC AND SOCIAL COST

The arms race produces many economic and social problems. The cost to the world in continued military expenditure of all kinds is calculated by the authoritative publication *World Military and Social Expenditures* at close to U.S. $1 trillion per year. This figure represents a slight decline over previous years: NATO's military expenditure for 1988 was three percent less than for 1987; in the Soviet Union and the Eastern European states, economic and political restructuring is beginning to take precedence over defence spending; Third World countries, burdened by famine and debt, are slowing down the military growth that characterized their economies in the 1980's. Nonetheless, global military expenditures still equal the total income for the poorest half of the world's population. Every two hours, the world spends on arms the equivalent of the annual budget of the United Nations Children's Fund (UNICEF).

Since World War II, world-wide military expenditures have increased, in real terms, between four and five times. They consume six percent of total world output, and throughout most of the 1980's rose at a faster rate than the economy generally. The six main military spenders – the U.S., USSR, U.K., France, China, and Federal Republic of Germany – account for more than 70 percent of the total. Developing countries spend 15 percent of the world total on arms, an amount they clearly cannot afford because it impedes their spending on health, education and other basics of development.

The full impact of the arms race is seen in how it uses up the physical and human resources of the world. Military research and development (R & D) nearly doubled in the 1980's and now accounts for more than a quarter of all R & D. A quarter of the world's scientists are engaged in military research. The big military spenders are the ones most heavily involved in the technological revolution for modernized missiles, spacecraft, electronics and aircraft. They are leading the way into a new generation of laser weapons and new "families of weapons" linked by high-speed computers. The risk of war by accident or miscalculation becomes greater each year despite the new communications linkages between Moscow and Washington. Some 60 to 80 million people world-wide are in military-related employment, of which 29 million are in armed forces. Of these, 11 million are in developed countries and 18 million spread around the much larger number of developing countries; at the same time, the developed countries remain much more militarized, employing in their forces twice the proportion of their populations as do the developing countries.

Most studies show that civilian R and D produces more commercial benefits in the world market. That route normally provides more flexibility in meeting consumer preferences. In general, evidence from national studies does not support the idea that high military spending is necessary for full employment. On the contrary, military spending contributes to unemployment by reducing public expenditures in labor-intensive sectors. The general tendency is for industries dependent on military contracts to employ fewer persons per unit of money invested in them. Non-military spending in the 1980's would have created more jobs than the prevailing level of military spending.

With the weight of governments behind it, the arms race competes strongly for natural, financial, human and technological resources that might otherwise be available for social and economic development. In short, the arms race absorbs far too great a proportion of resources and hinders international commerce, cooperation and confidence-building in a world where two-thirds of the population live with massive problems of underdevelopment. Heavy reliance on military technologies is an omen of future relative decline of a nation in the international economic system, which is a reason that both superpowers are under pressure from forces within their own societies to cut military spending.

In the Third World, reduced development influences regional conflicts which themselves threaten security. Africa, the Middle East, Latin America, and Asia are filled with examples of the suffering of people caused by deprivation, oppression, and uprooting. While the bulk of global spending is by the NATO and Warsaw Pact alliances, which has enormous ramifications for debt burdens, interest payments and lessened ability to meet social needs in developed countries, it is in developing countries that the crippling effects of high military spending are seen most graphically.

Some 33 major armed conflicts raged, mostly in Third World countries, in 1988, though by the end of the year this number was reduced to 28 through mutually agreed solutions in the Iraq-Iran, Ethiopia-Somalia and Chad-Libya conflicts and in Angola and Namibia. One of the 33 conflicts was in Europe (Northern Ireland), five were located in the Middle East, five in South Asia, six in Pacific Asia, eleven in Africa and five in Central and South America.

As a consequence of the spread of international violence and underdevelopment, the refugee problem has become increasingly acute, with the total number of refugees now soaring past 14.5 million, a significant increase from the 10 million refugees of the early 1980's. This index alone makes clear that the nations of the world have made little tangible progress in alleviating the human misery resulting from international conflict. The 150 regional conflicts since World War II have claimed more than 20 million lives, most of them civilian.

Though the trend of ever-increasing numbers of armed conflicts has reversed, the arms trade throughout the Third World has stabilized at the highest level ever at $32 billion. The duplicity of nations in simultaneously talking peace and feeding the arms race is nowhere more evident than in the global arms trade. The U.S. and the USSR account for two-thirds of this lucrative trade, which in effect con-tributes to the financing of the superpowers' own war machines. The Soviets, the largest exporter, sell arms principally to Angola, Cuba, India, Iraq, Libya and Syria. The Americans, who increased sales to the Third World 66 percent in 1988 over 1987, sell mostly to Egypt, Israel, Pakistan, Saudi Arabia and South Korea. Meanwhile, U.S. Secretary of State George Shultz went to the U.N. Third Special Session on Disarmament and complained that advanced weapons technology is spreading throughout the world and terrorists were making use of explosives and missiles. ". . . If we are not part of the solution, we are part of the problem," he said. At the same meeting, Soviet Foreign Minister Eduard Shevardnadze said, "One of the obstacles impeding settlement of regional conflicts is the intensive transfusion of weapons into zones of increased confrontation."

Overall, the Middle East is the largest arms market, receiving two-thirds of all weapons delivered to the Third World in the period 1985-88. China has become a major arms exporter, exceeding in 1988 the combined sales of Britain, Italy and the Federal Republic of Germany. Third World countries themselves are getting into the arms export trade, with Brazil, Egypt and North Korea now appearing in SIPRI's annual listing of the 15 major arms exporters. Sweden ranks ninth and Canada thirteenth (although Canadian sales fell off sharply between 1986 and 1988).

A U.N. register of arms transfers would at least put a global spotlight on the nefarious arms trade and enable the strengthening of regulations already adopted by many supplier countries. But the most the U.N. has been able to do, so far, is to establish an expert study to recommend measures to control the arms trade. Ironically, if East-West disarmament proceeds, the major suppliers will step up sales to the Third World to compensate military manufacturers for lessened domestic demand. Unless the major powers adopt serious measures to convert their defence industries into civilian production, the Third World will end up with more weapons than ever, acquired at firesale prices.

Militarism is one factor in the staggering debt crisis faced by Third World countries where the external debt has now reached $1.3 trillion (a one-third increase since 1982). But debt has deeper roots, traced to the inequities in the structural relationship between the industrialized countries of the North and the developing countries of the South. So skewed is this relationship that, in 1988, the net flow of money *from* the South *to* the North was $43 billion. This anomaly is caused by the interest payments on the existing debt load. The World Bank and the International Monetary Fund (IMF), established to assist development, are now net receivers from the poor, who borrowed so much in the first place because they could not get fair and stable prices for their exports of primary products or sufficient entry to the world trading systems or access to the scientific and technological advances that spurred Northern growth. African countries provide a telling example of the distress caused by these inequities. In order to get more foreign exchange revenues, some have switched from growing food for local consumption to cash crops for export. The inevitable consequence is food shortages.

Paradoxically, the wealthiest country, the United States, has become the world's largest debtor, a situation worsened by its huge military budget. The capital surplus countries, Japan and Germany, finance the U.S. deficit while the developing countries are starved for the capital which they desperately need in order to accelerate development and respond to urgent human need. Far from concern with development, the priority concentration of the North has been on military and geo-political objectives in the East-West competition. The countries of the Third World have frequently been regarded as arenas for the extension of the competition between the U.S. and the Soviet bloc and for their economic, cultural and ideological rivalry. The arms race particularly has pre-empted a large part of the world's resources away from development in the poorer regions.

The damage done to Third World indebted countries, particularly in Africa and Latin America, in attempting to meet the burden of debt payment is now widely recognized, but no comprehensive solution has been offered by the international financial system, which includes the IMF, the World Bank and the banking community, supported by Northern governments. The IMF, extending credits on a case-by-case basis, imposes such strict conditions, forcing cuts in government spending, that local investment for development is brought to a halt and even reversed. The debt trap is closed even tighter by the actions of the rich in developing countries who have sent so much of their capital abroad for safe-keeping, rather than invest it in their own countries. With the Baker Plan and the Brady Plan (named after James Baker and Nicholas Brady, successive U.S. Treasury Secretaries), the creditor nations have eased some of the pressure, but the poor still suffer from cutbacks because the North will not implement an integrated approach to debt recovery emphasizing human development priorities and growth with equity. The reason this does not happen is because the poor are politically powerless – a condition they are starting to break out of through food riots. Instability and crisis now dominate the most heavily-indebted countries: Argentina, Bolivia, Brazil, Chile, Colombia, Cote d' Ivoire, Ecuador, Mexico, Morocco, Nigeria, Peru, the Philippines, Uruguay, Venezuela and Yugoslavia.

Military spending compounds these development problems. Not many Third World governments risk dissatisfying the military with heavy cuts. The civilian budgets for housing, education and health are more vulnerable. And as these cuts are imposed, the need for the military to keep order of a sort grows. However, future progress will depend on the reduction of conflict. "Food wars" are the main cause of modern-day famines. This has been seen in the Sudan where supplies were disrupted as a means of intimidating the populace. In Cambodia, Mozambique and Angola, "scorched earth" policies of massacring peasants and ravishing crops have been carried out to cow people into submission.

The combination of high debt service and military expenditures is often devastating. In Pakistan, defence spending and debt servicing amount to 84 percent of earned government revenue. Similar discordancies are found in the Philippines and in Latin America. Reducing military expenditure is a necessary step to accelerating development in the South but is unlikely to occur until Northern governments seriously address the underlying economic and social disequilibriums in North-South relations. The 1989 summit of the seven major industrial nations, congratulating itself for progress, refused suggestions that it meet with several leaders from the South, who were on hand in Paris at the invitation of French President Mitterand.

The present distortions in the international system deplete scarce resources required to meet human needs: they leave 770 million people malnourished, 1.3 billion without access to safe drinking water, 100 million without adequate shelter, 880 million unable to read or write. And it is the children who suffer most of all, 14 million under the age of five dying each year for lack of elementary development needs. In South Asia, 75 million children under 14 work as virtual slaves. Millions more homeless "street children" throughout the Third World will increase with the rural-urban migration and other social strains on families. In the words of UNICEF's 1989 report: "It is the young child who is paying the highest of all prices, and who will bear the most recurring of all costs, for the mounting debt repayments, the drop in export earnings, the increase in food costs, the fall in family incomes, the rundown of health services, the narrowing of educational opportunities."

The vicious circle of increased arms, stifled development, and growing global instability and insecurity continues.

The projections are even more alarming. The growth and distribution of disadvantaged populations and environmental damage are now inter-related. While much environmental damage is attributed to the reckless use and misuse of resources in the richer parts of the world, the combination of poverty and rapid population growth in developing countries is also a major factor. In order to survive, the growing numbers of poor people in developing countries are forced into a ferocious assault on their environment. A deteriorating rural environment, in which water, fuel, wood, and agricultural resources are used up, is a principal cause of urban growth. Massive urban consumption of resources and production of waste worsen environmental pollution.

The U.N.'s *State of the World 1989 Population Report* estimates that world population will increase by over 90 million people each year until 2000 – all but six million occurring in developing countries. The population at the end of this century is certain to be at least 6.25 billion and even optimistic levelling-off projections have the population reaching 8.5 billion by 2025. That is to say, in 35 years the world will have to feed, shelter, educate, and provide health care for a 61 percent increase in the human family, the overwhelming number of whom will live in lands that are even now unable to meet the basic human needs of their populations.

The trend lines of deforestation, ozone depletion, soil erosion and diminishment of plant species are all getting worse at the present level of population. The increase in population will compound these dangers. Then, to bring the Third World up to European and North American standards will exacerbate the problems. There are grave doubts that the world's ecosystem has the capacity to sustain a five-to-tenfold increase in demand. Air, water and soil are not limitless and we are poisoning all three today.

According to the Food and Agriculture Organization of the United Nations (FAO), it is already apparent that by 2000, the lands of most developing countries will scarcely be able to feed their expected populations if traditional farming methods are continued. Two-fifths of their land area, with 60 percent of their total population, will be inhabited by more people than can be supported. One of the most disturbing features of this scenario is that population growth will be fastest precisely in those areas where land resources are least capable of meeting human needs and where the risk of desertification and fuel-wood deficiency is highest.

The FAO, working with limited resources to modernize agriculture in the developing countries, warns that actions taken over the next 40 years will be crucial to human history. The next four decades will determine whether populations can be accommodated without widespread suffering from hunger, poverty, conflict and irreversible degradation of the environment. The FAO maintains: "The outcome of current trends concerns not only the potentially critical countries but the entire human race."

On its present course, the world is inexorably moving to the anarchy foreseen by Secretary-General Perez de Cuellar.

Chapter Two

The 1990's: Disarmament, Development, Environmental Action

Several years ago, during a tour of villages in Bangladesh to study development, I encountered a mother of eight children. Most of the children were naked and one of them particularly caught my eye, a boy about eight with the right side of his face blackened as the result of a birth injury. Because I was accompanied by a female social worker, the woman invited me into her hut. The dwelling was built of clay and mud with a grass roof. There was no electricity. The nearest water was several hundred metres away. Long sticks of cow dung were drying, to be used as fuel. A pot of date palm juice, which flows from trees like maple syrup, was being heated over a fire.

As we sat on plain wood chairs, the woman told me about her life. She was married at 13. Her husband works as a sharecropper on the land. There was enough basic food at the present time, although the children's faces and bellies clearly revealed nutritional deficiencies. A one-room school was two kilometres away. Finally, I asked the woman what she wanted in life. She looked at the ground for a moment, then raised her head and said, "I would like enough food for my children every day and a good school for them."

That women spoke for the hundreds of millions of people in the Third World who are trapped in endless cycles of poverty. When I met her in 1976, Bangladesh, the most densely populated country in the world, had 80 million people. Only 40 percent of the population received sufficient protein, 80 percent were illiterate, and over a third of the workforce consisted of landless labourers earning 40 cents for a day's work. Today, the population of Bangladesh is 110 million, and life is actually worse, since the flooding of its two huge rivers, the Ganges and the Brahmaputra, two years in a row has caused catastrophic damage. In 1988, floodwaters inundated 84 percent of the land area, dislocating 45 million people and causing 2,500 deaths. Crops were devastated, water systems polluted and diarrheal diseases swept the nation that has only one hospital bed for every 3,583 persons and one physician for 6,252. More than half the population lives below the Bangladesh poverty line. The government devotes 18 percent of its national budget to defence.

The flooding problem begins outside Bangladesh in the rivers' watersheds in northern India, Nepal and Bhutan, where the Himalayan hillsides have been ravaged by deforestation. With the denuded soil no longer able to absorb monsoon rains, the runoff increases, bringing with it ever larger loads of silt that ends up on the river bottoms of Bangladesh. Huge reforestation and dike systems are needed. Bangladesh is a prime example of the interlocking problems of development and the environment beyond the solution of a single country. The 1989 summit of the seven major industrial nations called for "coordinated action by the international community."

The poverty in a Bangladesh village may seen a long way from the disarmament conference rooms of the United Nations. But any discussion of security today must encompass the daily needs of untold millions whose deprivation is a growing source of conflicts in many regions. There is a connection between over-armament and under-development. Competitive arms races breed insecurity among nations. Scarce resources misdirected to arms contribute further to insecurity. The scale of poverty and environmental degradation now require urgent action. The first priority must be to cut back on weapons production, a global sickness that is literally robbing the poor of their right to a life of decency. For one billion people, security is measured in their daily struggle for survival. On top of this, planetary life-support systems are under severe stress. All the resources of the world are needed to address these global crises. We can no longer afford militarism.

It is not possible to establish overnight a new system of global security, but it may be possible by the year 2000 if the political processes are infused with an enlightened attitude. Our task today is to build a bridge to 2000: a bridge with three pillars, disarmament, development and environment. We cannot afford to wait until all the pieces of a new concept of global security are fitted together. The agenda for the 1990's must concentrate on building the three pillars.

DISARMAMENT.

The most pressing work in disarmament in the 1990's will be to strengthen the Non-Proliferation Treaty (NPT); negotiate a Comprehensive Test Ban (CTB); cut the strategic nuclear arsenals of the U.S. and Soviet Union by at least 50 percent and curb modernization; have all nuclear powers adopt a no-first-use policy; reduce conventional forces in Europe; and complete a world-wide treaty eliminating chemical weapons.

The first two, NPT and CTB, go together even though the Western powers are trying to separate them.

The NPT came into force two decades ago with the aim of stopping the spread of nuclear weapons from nuclear to non-nuclear countries; beginning the process of disarmament in the nuclear countries; and guaranteeing all nations access to nuclear technology for peaceful purposes. It was to go until 1995 with a review every five years. To date, 140 nations have signed, making it the most widely supported arms control treaty in existence. But there are important hold-outs including the very countries widely believed to have nuclear weapons capability: India, Pakistan, Argentina, Brazil, Israel and South Africa. France and China, have not signed, though both state they adhere to it.

In return for countries not acquiring nuclear weapons, the nuclear weapons countries agreed to pursue negotiations to cease the arms race. Article VI is central to this commitment. It reads:

Each of the parties to the Treaty undertakes to pursue negotiations in good faith on effective measures relating to cessation of the nuclear arms race at an early date and to nuclear disarmament, and on a treaty on general and complete disarmament under strict and effective international control.

This was the basis of the NPT bargain. "Measures relating to cessation of the nuclear arms race" was intended to cover such measures as a CTB, a ban on the production of fissionable material for weapons, a freeze on the production of additional nuclear weapons, and a ban on flight testing of delivery vehicles. Although a CTB itself would not stop the nuclear arms race, it is clear that there can be no cessation without it. Nuclear testing is key to the development of new weapon systems. Reductions in arms while nations continue to test and modernize is not "cessation." A smaller number of more modern nuclear weapons, made more accurate and effective through testing, would, in effect, accelerate the arms race. That is exactly what is happening today.

A CTB has been a long sought-after goal. The U.S., supported by the U.K., entered into negotiations with the Soviet Union during the 1970's for a CTB. Those negotiations recessed in 1979. The Reagan Administration lowered the priority for a CTB, setting it only as a "long-range" goal. In 1983, the U.S. stated that tests were required for development, modernization and certification of warheads. It was also apparent that continued testing was needed for the development of the Strategic Defense Initiative. Throughout the 1980's, the U.S. voted "no" on U.N. resolutions dealing with a CTB and has blocked negotiations at the Conference on Disarmament. Testing continues and the superpowers now have six times the number of strategic nuclear weapons they possessed when the NPT was signed.

In 1987, the U.S. agreed to join with the USSR in a joint verification experiment to monitor each other's tests. This would enable the U.S. to ratify the 1974 Threshold Test Ban Treaty (TTBT) and the 1976 Peaceful Nuclear Explosions Treaty (PNET). These treaties are outdated because of their excessively high threshold of 150 kilotonnes; actually, scientists have developed seismic verification techniques to the point where it is possible to detect, through a global network, explosions down to one kilotonne. Anything less than one kilotonne has virtually no military significance.

The importance of a CTB is growing, not lessening. Under a CTB, neither the U.S. nor the Soviet Union would be able to develop new "third generation" nuclear weapons such as the x-ray laser and other exotic nuclear weapons that depend on directing energy generated by nuclear blasts. Such a restriction would foreclose an even more expensive arms race.

The non-nuclear weapons states claim they are being discriminated against in what amounts to a double standard in world politics. Charges that the nuclear weapons' powers are in flagrant breach of their obligations have been made repeatedly at the NPT review conferences. The non-nuclear weapons states have sent a strong message to the nuclear parties that they must abide by their treaty obligations to halt and reverse the nuclear arms race if the NPT is to endure. The 1995 review will determine the future of the NPT. If there is no CTB by that date, the NPT may break down, opening the door to a full-scale effort by two dozen nations to acquire nuclear weapons.

The gravity of this situation has led to a "crash programme" by some 40 states to raise public consciousness on the issue and press the nuclear states into negotiations. In 1963, President John F. Kennedy and Soviet leader Nikita Khrushchev signed the Partial Test Ban Treaty (PTBT) which banned nuclear explosions in the atmosphere, outer space and under water, leaving underground as the only permissible testing place. It was successful as a health measure, but the superpowers proceeded to conduct underground tests at a faster pace than the previous atmospheric tests.

Disillusioned by the failure of the nuclear powers to live up to their promises, a movement was started by non-nuclear parties to the

PTBT to take advantage of a provision that allows them to call for an amendment conference. Led by Indonesia, Mexico, Peru, Sri Lanka, Venezuela and Yugoslavia, the group proposed in 1987 that a PTBT amendment conference be convened at some later date to convert the PTBT into a CTB. The Soviet Union supported the proposal, but the U.S., U.K., and France opposed it, most of the Western states (including Canada) abstaining. The move was enthusiastically welcomed by most of the U.N. General Assembly. The U.S. and U.K., as depository states for the PTBT, had no choice but to agree to plan the conference, which will be held in the early 1990's. But they are are likely to exercise their right to veto the outcome.

The Western states will argue that the NPT should not be jeopardized because it ensures the peaceful use of atomic energy. A protracted battle can be expected. The non-nuclear states will generate strong pressure on the U.S. and U.K. Given the adamant pro-testing stance of the U.S. and the reaffirmed policy of NATO that it must modernize short-range nuclear weapons, an abrupt change of policy by the West seems unlikely. A compromise, lowering the testing limit, is possible. But unless the limit is set no higher than two kilotonnes, the compromise will undermine the quest for a CTB.

The surest way to preserve and strengthen the NPT is to put a CTB in place. Moreover, this is precisely the way to shut off nuclear development in the near-nuclear states, since Argentina, Brazil, India, Israel, Pakistan and South Africa are all parties to the PTBT and would be bound by the amendment. Thus the actions of the 1990's will determine whether the arms race is shut off by both a CTB and NPT or whether the world will be deprived of both instruments of disarmament.

Obviously, the progress made in the bilateral negotiations to reduce strategic nuclear weapons will have a strong psychological bearing on the future of the NPT. Attaining the declared 50 percent cut is unlikely and even if it is reached, the intention to keep modernizing nuclear weapons will vitiate the achievement in the eyes of the near-nuclear weapons states. The U.K., France and China will not even begin to look at cutting their stocks until the superpowers reduce far more than 50 percent. The opponents of the NPT will continue to claim that it is discriminatory.

In the 1990's, the eye must be kept firmly fixed on what is politically possible. Some significant cuts in the strategic arsenals of the U.S. and Soviet Union are politically possible, provided a longstanding dispute over the Anti-Ballistic Missile (ABM) Treaty is resolved. The Soviets maintain that testing new ballistic missile defence technologies, the object of the U.S. SDI programme, is prohibited by the ABM. The U.S., however, is pursuing the programme, even though the funding has been scaled back. The overwhelming weight of scientific opinion is that there are no effective means of defending populations from ballistic missile attack and that none is in prospect. Given this scientific reality, a mutual reaffirmation of the ABM Treaty for at least the next decade would clear the way for significant strategic cuts.

Similarly, it is politically possible – and urgent – to make deep cuts in conventional forces in Europe and complete a chemical weapons ban in the early years of the next decade. Gorbachev's acceptance of the principle of asymmetrical cuts in Europe (the Soviets would cut much larger numbers than the West because of their numerical superiority), combined with his unilateral implementation of cuts in forward-based troops and equipment, set the stage for the new 23-nation Conventional Forces in Europe (CFE) forum, which opened in Vienna in 1989.

The mandate is to reach agreement between the 16 members of NATO and the seven members of the Warsaw Pact on reducing the number of soldiers and non-nuclear weapons across all Europe, "from the Atlantic to the Urals," to an approximation of parity. A sense of urgency has been introduced in the negotiation, producing optimism that an early agreement can be reached that will constrain each side's ability to launch an attack.

Considering the gridlock that characterized, over a 14-year period, the previous East-West conventional force negotiations in Vienna, the new forum offers a great deal of hope. The historic achievement of any significant cuts on both sides should not be discounted. But even if deep cuts are attained, East and West would each still have 1.35 million troops pitted against each other, 20,000 tanks, between 16,500 and 24,000 pieces of artillery, 28,000 armored vehicles and between 1,500 and 3,800 aircraft.

Significant conventional cuts in Europe are inescapably tied to the presence of short-range nuclear forces (SNF). Gorbachev wants to negotiate these down to zero. NATO is split on the issue, with West Germany and some of the smaller NATO partners strongly in favour of eliminating SNF, while the U.S., U.K. and France are opposed and insist on developing a new Lance weapon that would have a range four times greater than the present one. The argument runs that, if war should break out, it would be more plausible for NATO to use this "lesser" nuclear weapon than call out the strategic forces. A crisis at the 1989 NATO summit was averted only after the two camps agreed to negotiate a partial reduction once a conventional force reduction agreement is signed and implemention started. The language of the 1989 NATO policy, contained in a document known as "A Comprehensive Concept of Arms Control and Disarmament," harps once more on nuclear weapons as deterrence:

> *For the foreseeable future, deterrence requires an appropriate mix of adequate and effective nuclear and conventional forces which will continue to be kept up to date where necessary. . . . Conventional defence alone cannot, however, ensure deterrence. Only the nuclear element can confront an aggressor with an unacceptable risk and thus plays an indispensable role in our current strategy of war prevention . . . The principles underlying the strategy of deterrence are of enduring validity.*

This is a policy of confrontation, not cooperation. It flies in the face of growing public sentiment in Europe opposed to the continued presence of nuclear weapons on European soil. If conventional force reductions are achieved, there is no reason not to proceed with the elimination of SNF.

For years, the Soviet Union and its allies have maintained a no-first-use policy. But the official U.S. position has been that such a policy would require massive build-ups in Western conventional capability. The West has always insisted on its right to turn to nuclear weapons in the event of a massive conventional attack by the Soviet bloc in Europe. If conventional parity is achieved in Europe, what excuse can NATO use to maintain its policy of using nuclear weapons first if the Soviets launch a conventional attack? With massive reductions, not build-ups, contemplated, now is the time for the West to pledge no-first-use. The present Western policy fuels the arms race, encourages the military establishment to believe in war-fighting strategies, and raises the spectre of a nuclear war. It will become increasingly difficult for NATO to hold to its deterrence policy in a world coming to recognize that nuclear weapons are an impediment to the full blossoming of the new East-West relationship.

At least 20 nations now possess the capacity to build lethal chemical weapons, with the two superpowers maintaining large stocks. Chemical weapons were used repeatedly in the Iran-Iraq war. Negotiations on a treaty prohibiting the production, stockpiling and transfer of chemical weapons have been conducted at the Conference on Disarmament in Geneva for seven years. With an agreement by the U.S. and Soviet Union on verification measures and a timetable for destroying stocks, the way is now clear to conclude the multilateral treaty. However, the continued nuclear arms race between the superpowers means that the demand from the smaller states that chemical disarmament proceed only in tandem with nuclear disarmament has not been met. Both big and small states need to be persuaded not to lose the current opportunity to rid the earth of chemical arms.

As the 1990's progress, a fundamental question will come into sharp focus: Why should some countries always have nuclear weapons while others never have them?

DEVELOPMENT

A discussion of development must first center on the meaning of the word, for it is used in very different contexts. By development I mean a process in which a person has the economic basis and freedom to develop his or her true potential in keeping with the common good. The development of the human being does indeed have a deeper dimension than economic, but without access to food, shelter, education, employment and health care there can be no full development. By this standard, more than one billion people are impoverished.

Over half live in the populous regions of South Asia and East Asia, concentrated in rural regions with high population density such as the Gangetic Plain of India, the delta region of Bangladesh, the island of Java in Indonesia and Central Mindanao in the Philippines. Extreme poverty is extensive in the resource-poor areas in western India and North-Western China. It is largely a rural phenomenon in Sub-Saharan Africa where poor, fragile soils and underdeveloped farming techniques predominate. In Latin America rural landlessness arises more from inequalities in land-holding than population pressures, while in urban areas poverty exists in massive ghettos. Additional millions live in absolute poverty in North Africa, the Middle East and the resource-poor areas in western Pakistan. Malnutrition, precarious housing, inadequate access to basic health and education facilities, insecure and badly paid jobs are the condition of life for these people. Among the undernourished, calorie intake is lowest for women and children.

Because food security can only be attained through raising the level of people's incomes, there is a real risk that in the 1990's the number of malnourished will continue to grow substantially. In the 1980's, their number grew five times faster than in the 1970's. In the past decade in Africa, for example, drought, famine and wars have created more than four million refugees and up to 11 million other displaced people.

The world economy functioned dangerously in the 1980's. The international monetary regime envisioned by the Bretton Woods agreement has collapsed. There has been an overdependence on international capital markets to regulate capital flows, a system which has worked badly. Eight economic regional giants – Japan, the U.S. (the Free-Trade Agreement makes Canada part of this bloc), the European Community, a group of Latin American countries, the Soviet-Comecon countries, Asian, China and India – control trade and shut out the bottom 20 percent of the world, including Africa. These industrial blocs are setting aside the problems of the poorest regions in order to deal with their own compelling problems. Aid is stagnant and the poorest countries are left to forage as best they can. In terms of economic growth, the 1980's has been a lost decade for most of the developing world. High interest rates, falling commodity prices, large debt burdens, volatile exchange rates and restricted markets have plagued their economies.

There are however, positive developments taking place which can lead to a stronger future. We can discern the following: a gradual converging of economic strategies; lessening of East-West confrontation; an opening toward greater popular participation in development; an awakening to the importance of environmentally sustainable development; a new understanding that human goals must be given a higher priority in the development process.

It is in this last area that the greatest progress needs to be made in the 1990's. But the prospects for making human and social development an integral part of economic policy are slim. Market-driven economies are the principal reason why such disparaties between the North and South exist in the first place. Development in its holistic sense has certainly never been the goal of the capital markets. Yet even this profit-first orientation is undergoing some modification as the result of the disequilibrium which characterizes North-South relations. Though re-structuring of the international economic system is necessary to fulfill the conditions for global security, this is a long-range goal at best. Meanwhile, it is better, for the sake of the millions of destitute, to get on with adjustment programmes to energize human development.

EDUCATION. In the past 40 years, adult literacy rates in the developing world have doubled from 30 to 60 percent. That is the good news. The bad news is that the remaining 40 percent will be the hardest to reach because the low-income countries have cut their education budgets in half as they struggle with the structural adjustments to their debt-ridden economies and the growth of military expenditures.

While dollars spent on a power plant or a port can yield a high return, investments in teachers and schools can yield an ever higher return.

HEALTH AND NUTRITION. Life expectancy in the developing countries is rising, but is still far short of the 76 years in the industrialized countries. Similarly, infant mortality in the low-income countries has been gradually declining, reaching 6.9 percent, but is still far above the one per cent reported by the industrialized countries. U.N. development workers have been able to bring safe drinking water to half a billion people and a quarter of a billion have been supplied with new sanitation facilities. Yet 1.2 billion people are still without safe drinking water and nearly two billion still have their health threatened by the lack of sanitary facilities. Three-quarters of the health problems in the developing world could be solved by a combination of prevention and cure: enough of the right food, clean water to drink, safe sanitation, access to family planning, immunization, and around 200 basic drugs. Diverting even part of military expenditures to development would make this programme affordable.

EMPLOYMENT. Because of population growth, it is estimated that over the next two decades, developing countries will need to create 700 million jobs – more jobs than currently exist in the entire industrialized world. The developing countries must bear the major burden of creating new jobs, but they can do so only if they can manufacture more goods which can be sold abroad. The full range of trade, financial, marketing and credit services must be extended to them. The walls of protectionism, built by the big trading blocs, must come down. Incentives such as market-based prices, equitable tax systems, and rational import and export controls are needed to encourage people to move into productive endeavours. The result will be farming, commercial and industrial activities that produce more goods and services for the developing countries.

POLITICAL AND ECONOMIC RIGHTS. People must have a democratic voice in their own development. As well as political freedom, people must have the economic freedom to participate in their own development – the freedom to be entrepreneurs. The private sector, if directed in a less exploitative manner, could be a potent engine for development. It could unleash the dynamism, creativity and talent of individuals throughout the world. Human capacity is the most important resource that a country possesses. Japan has very few natural resources, yet it is the fastest-growing large industrialized country in the world.

POPULATION CONTROL. Because the rate of growth of population is so high in the most disadvantaged areas, successful development is inextricably tied to family planning. It is tempting to place blame for population problems on the developing countries; yet it is the rich, more than the poor, who are straining the earth's carrying capacities. The typical North American infant will consume some 15 to 20 times more of the globe's economic output than a child in the Third World. A more equitable sharing of world resources must figure in long-range population solutions. But the immediate problem of over-crowding and resource squeeze remains.

Though rapid economic and social development is a prerequisite to population control, family planning must be a part of that process. Otherwise, the sheer momentum of population growth will over-whelm the development process. U.N. projections that world popula-tion will stop growing at ten billion, about double the present size, a century from now assume that fertility in the developing countries will drop by a third in the next 30 to 40 years. This in turn assumes that a very large number of women in the developing countries will start to use family planning in the next two decades. If this does not happen, the less optimistic projections show a population already approaching ten billion by 2025. By that time Africa's population would be nearly 2 billion and Asia's 5.5 billion, bigger than the population of the whole world today. These figures, and their implications for the future, should be enough to make it clear that the population crisis is a matter for action now, not next century.

Dramatic progress can be made, as Brazil has shown in cutting the fertility rate, 5.75 children per woman in 1970, to 3.2 today. Brazil will probably end this century with 170 million people, 50 million fewer than demographers predicted a decade ago. Fertility rates are also declining in many areas as the result of family-planning pro-grammes, but there are still many countries in Africa, the Middle East and Asia where the vast majority of people have no access to modern family planning techniques. There is a pressing need for contraceptive availability. If it is not met, the already excessive rate of abortions will grow as a reflection of unmet family-planning needs. Reductions in fertility have been found to be closely related to the strength of family planning programmes. Although the world now spends around $3 billion annually on family planning services for developing countries, half of this is accounted for by China and India. And in the 1980's, most Third World governments cut back budgets for social services.

Examining the magnitude of all the development problems to-day, William Draper, administrator of the United Nations Develop-ment Programme, has called for a new Marshall Plan financed by the industrialized nations and focussed on the poorest countries. More than 40 years ago, the United States launched the Marshall Plan, a far-sighted programme to rebuild war-torn Europe. The Marshall Plan was an infusion of capital into countries that already had a human resources infrastructure. Today an infusion of capital must be used to develop the human brain power, skills and energy of the people. Third World countries must be enabled to do this job themselves. They must train, nurture and develop teachers, nurses, technicians and administrators in their own way. The industrialized North can best help this occur by removing the obstacles to development, the staggering debt, unstable commodity prices and discriminatory trading rules.

ENVIRONMENT

In 1987, a remarkable document caught the attention of the world. Called *Our Common Future,* it was the report of the World Commission on Environment and Development, headed by Prime Minister Gro Harlem Brundtland of Norway, the only national environment minister ever to become head of government. The independent commission, comprising 23 experts, was established by the United Nations to propose long-term environmental strategies for achieving sustainable development by the year 2000 and beyond. The report spelled out how the Earth's atmosphere is being changed at an unprecedented rate by pollutants resulting from human activities, inefficient and wasteful fossil fuel use and the effects of rapid population growth in many areas. These changes represent a major threat to international security and are already having harmful consequences over many parts of the globe. A global call to action was issued for Third World development strategies to promote a better life without further degradation of the environment. That is what "sustainable development" means.

A sea-change in public attitude towards the environment is now occurring. When the U.N. held the first of a series of international conferences on global problems in 1972, concentrating on environmental deterioration, the general public was virtually oblivious to the dangers. Since then, the public has developed a deep concern about the condition of the planet, and national ministries for the environment have been established. The greening of politicians is well under way with one leader after another making sharp U-turns in putting environmental concerns high on their policy agendas.

The sudden emergence of "green" issues, from the dumping of toxic waste to the sinking of a Soviet nuclear submarine off Norway, coincides with the decline in East-West tensions and a shift away from fears about the danger of war in Europe. In 1989, *Time* magazine presented a picture of the globe wrapped in polyethylene in place of its usual Man of the Year. A five-hour television concert, inspired by the Brundtland Report, was shown around the world. Protest songs and rock videos, raging about the world's ills from contaminated food and water to ozone depletion, from the destruction of rain forests to nuclear weapons, reflect the alienation so many young people feel today. The angry voices of rock music have joined the abstract findings of elite conferences in a common appeal to stop deterioration and protect the atmosphere before it is too late.

Actually, there is nothing elitist about the inter-relationship of energy, ecology, population and development. The connections are now dramatized in the destruction of forests for fuel, a carbon dioxide buildup responsible for global warming, the migration of peoples forced by a spread of deserts, and the choking off of basic development programmes by the Third World debt crisis. Present patterns of energy consumption, essentially the use of fossil fuels such as coal, oil and gas, are a central cause of the increasing greenhouse effect. Ecological refugees will mount into the hundreds of millions if a rise in sea level, now predicted over the next few decades, results in massive inundation with a consequent loss of food production.

The Interaction Council, a group of 20 former heads of government, warns:

> *The cost of inaction now will become staggering a few years hence, triggering political tensions and conflicts hitherto unknown. If humankind continues along its present path, huge imbalances in economic wealth aggravated by population growth in the various regions of the world, may become a source of conflict possibly degenerating into war.*

An international conference in 1988, sponsored by the Canadian government, called for a global reduction of carbon dioxide emissions by 20 percent by 2005. However, most experts consider such a reduction as insufficient to stop global warming: a 50-percent reduction is needed. And with China and India using ever greater amounts of coal, the prospect for major reduction is slight.

While the environment problem is often focussed on the Third World, the main responsibility for global environmental deterioration lies with the industrial countries. They have been the major sources of greenhouse effects. Cheap fuel enabled industrialization in the North to take place. Clearly, the industrialized countries must take the

lead in committing themselves to meaningful targets in order to in-
duce complementary action by the developing countries. The industrialized countries' dumping of toxic wastes in Third World countries
(desperate for the revenue obtained) should obviously be banned immediately.

A safe and sustainable energy future must rely on new thinking
and new approaches in all countries. A shift in the fossil fuel mix from
coal and oil to gas and the introduction of renewable sources of energy on a large scale are required. Although nuclear energy avoids
carbon dioxide emissions, it cannot be considered as the principal
solution to the warming crisis because of the risks and cost of permanent disposal of spent fuel rods. On the other hand, a shut-off of
nuclear reactors would at present lead to increased use of coal and
gas. More effective internationally binding rules governing the management of nuclear energy as well as carbon dioxide will have to be
accepted by all nations.

It is in the Third World that the effects of environmental damage
are felt most grievously. Tropical forests are being felled at the rate of
11 million hectares a year; top soil is being washed away by wind and
rain at the rate of 26 billion tonnes a year; new stretches of desert are
appearing at the rate of six million hectares a year; and build-up of salt
and stagnant water threaten half of the world's irrigated cropland.
Nowhere are environmental conditions so appalling as in the slums of
the big cities. Before 2000, the urban population of the developing
world is expected to swell by 750 million people. Seventeen of the 23
cities with populations exceeding 10 million will be in the Third
World. Just to maintain today's marginal standards, most countries
will have to expand such urban services as water, sanitation, transportation and communications by 65 percent.

The effects are felt most acutely at the lowest level – by the poorest, least powerful and mainly women. It is they who have to walk
further and further each year to fetch firewood from the dwindling
woodlands; they who must search for hours for a stretch of unpol-
luted water; they who must cope with the effects of environmental
degradation on their own and their family's health.

Though the demands of rural people are responsible for much of
the damage, the biggest culprits are deforestation for logging and land
clearing for cash crops. In Central America, cattle ranchers are responsible for felling 20,000 square kilometres of forest a year since the late
1970's. Bringing in the best land for cash-crops forced many families
onto more fragile marginal land in the first place. Land hunger, scarce
fuel, pollution and migration deepen the poor's sense of uncertainty

about the future. Already, many are being forced into actions that they know are likely further to jeopardise their security. For example, women use manure as a fuel instead of fertilizer – mortgaging tomorrow's food to cook today's.

The Brundtland report emphasizes that four of the most urgent global requirements – relating to tropical forests, water, desertification and population – could be funded with the equivalent of less than one month's global military spending. The recent destruction of much of Africa's dry land agricultural production was more severe than if an invading army had pursued a scorched-earth policy. "Yet most of the affected governments still spend far more to protect their people from invading armies than from invading desert," Brundtland said. The connection between the environment and militarism is much more than financial. For already in parts of Latin America, Asia, the Middle East and Africa, environmental decline is becoming a source of political unrest and international tension. The Horn of Africa and Central America are cases in point. The fundamental causes of conflicts there have been as much environmental as political, stemming from lack of resources in over-crowded lands. Resource scarcities and ecological stresses threaten the security of people and nations; as situations deteriorate, military force is often used in response to a non-military threat. Millions of refugees fleeing war and famine compound international tensions. As a minimum to start the 1990's, governments should assess the cost-effectiveness, in terms of achieving security, of money spent on armaments compared with money spent on reducing poverty or restoring a ravaged environment.

With recommendations for better use of population and human resources, food security, energy and industrial conservation and international cooperation, Brundtland points the way to a global transition to a sustainable future. The report's chief value, however, is in demonstrating the interlocking nature of the world crises of the arms race, poverty and environmental degradation. The crises are all one. "Ecology and economy are becoming ever more interwoven – locally, regionally, nationally and globally – into a seamless net of causes and effects." The onus for solution lies with no one group of nations. All nations would suffer from the disappearance of rain forests in the tropics, the loss of plant and animal species, and changes in rainfall patterns; all nations suffer from the release of gases damaging the ozone layer; all nations would suffer from a nuclear war. National boundaries have become so porous that traditional distinctions between local, national and international issues have become blurred. A greatly strengthened international system has now become essential.

★ ★ ★

In summation, the bridge to 2000 requires three strong pillars: disarmament, development, environmental protection. The priority issues are now identified for the 1990's agenda:

- Deep cuts in nuclear and conventional forces are politically possible. The Non-Proliferation Treaty can only be saved by a Comprehensive Test Ban.
- The obstacles to development in the Third World, the staggering debt, unstable commodity prices and discriminatory trade rules, must be removed by the industrialized countries. Development programmes must emphasize the health and education needs of people.
- Global development must be harmonized with environmental maintenance: protecting the atmosphere and oceans and countering deforestation. Both industrialized and developing countries need to work in partnership to secure sustainable economic growth and a more equitable distribution of income and resources to alleviate debilitating poverty.

Chapter Three

2000 and Beyond:
The Road to Common Security

The 1990's bridge must have a destination: a new framework for global security. The system of collective security laid down in the Charter of the United Nations provides the basis for this development. But the Charter alone is not enough. The experience of the 1980's with its dramatic examples of arms build-ups, massive poverty and environmental deterioration shows the need to create a world order in which international peace rests on a commitment to cooperative management of the planet. Just as no municipality or township, let alone a country, would dream of carrying out its responsibilities for good order without regulations and structures to enforce them, so too the world must have a system of law which nations cooperate in establishing.

No one would willingly live in a community where the neighbours on both sides filled their homes with explosives and trained their arsenals of weapons on each other. Yet that is how we are living in the global community. The nation-state was created to ensure security. But the nuclear age and the interdependent economic and environmental systems have swept by the nation-state. No nation today can assure its own security by threatening the security of others. Common security is the only security. That is the lesson of the 1980's, not yet ready to be accepted as the 1990's open, but essential if the 21st century is to know any true human security anywhere.

The formulation for an approach to common security has been building up for some time. In 1971, a commission of distinguished world leaders, headed by Lester B. Pearson, former Prime Minister of Canada and Nobel Peace Laureate, issued the first major political statement that peace can only be ensured by overcoming world hunger, mass misery and the vast disparities between rich and poor. Their report, *Partners in Development,* called for a more coordinated international approach to stimulate aid and development policies. The Pearson Commission set an aid target of 0.7 percent of gross national product (GNP) of developed countries to be transferred to developing countries as official development assistance (ODA). Over the next 19 years, only Sweden, the Netherlands, Norway and Denmark reached the target; the average of the donor countries is 0.35 percent. The Pearson strategy went far beyond aid with these major recommendations: create a framework for free and equitable international trade; promote mutually beneficial flows of foreign private investment; meet the problem of mounting debts; slow the growth of population.

The beginnings of what would become known as the New International Economic Order, adopted at the U.N. in 1974, but later discarded, were contained in the Pearson Report. Looking back on the 1970s, it was a time of wrenching change in the way we think about the world and our place in it. The global economic upheaval of the early part of the decade confirmed for the developing countries that the existing economic system did not work in their interests. World poverty came to be seen as the result of a complex and unjust economic system rather than the simple product of "backwardness." Developing countries bonded together into the Group of 77 to try to pressure the developed countries for a better deal on trade and commodity issues. The Organization of Petroleum Exporting Countries (OPEC) suddenly struck with steep rises in oil prices; the balance of power began to shift and the industrialized countries went on the defensive, fearing their loss of control over the resources and regulation of world development. The 1970's closed with an effort to move from confrontation to negotiation, but the chaos in the world order proved overpowering. Piece-meal approaches to mounting problems continued.

At the start of the 1980's, another high-level international commission led by Willy Brandt, former Chancellor of the Federal Republic of Germany and also a Nobel Peace Laureate, published a report on international development. This time North-South issues were joined to the East-West conflict: reshaping world-wide North-South relations is crucial to the future of humankind and equal in importance to stopping the arms race. This would be "the greatest challenge to mankind for the remainder of this century." The report, *North-South: A Programme for Survival*, stimulated the unprecedented North-South summit of 22 world leaders, co-chaired by President Lopez Portillo of Mexico and Prime Minister Pierre Trudeau of Canada, who met in Cancun, Mexico in 1981. Although Cancun produced a bland roster of good intentions, its chief value was in putting world poverty on the international political agenda.

Insisting that the world faced "much greater dangers" than at any time since World War II, Brandt called for a fundamental change in relations between North and South as well as between East and West. The world is a unity, he said, and we must begin to act as fellow members who depend on one another. To promote genuine development and self-sustaining growth, the Commission set out a programme of priorities: a major initiative in favour of the poverty belts of Africa and Asia; measures for international food security; a Common Fund to stabilize primary commodity exports; reversal of the trend of protecting Northern industries against competition from the Third World; improved international investment regulation to enable developing countries to benefit from the resources of trans-national corporations; reform of the monetary system to relate Special Drawing Rights to the financial needs of the South; broadening of the international financial structures, and a World Development Fund leading eventually to a system of international taxation. Brandt also linked the high spending on arms with the low spending on measures to end hunger and ill-health in the Third World.

This latter theme was the focal point for a U.N. expert study on disarmament and development, headed by Inga Thorsson, Sweden's Under-Secretary of State, which concluded: "The world has a choice. It can continue to pursue the arms race or it can move with deliberate speed towards a more sustainable economic and political order. It cannot do both." By taking a broader approach to the problem of security, the Thorsson group defined a "dynamic triangular relationship" between disarmament, development and security. The purpose of national security is to secure the independence and sovereignty of the nation-state, the freedom and the means to develop economically, socially and culturally, which is precisely what is meant by development. Security is threatened by a reduction in economic growth, ecological stresses and resource scarcities, and morally unacceptable and politically hazardous polarization of wealth and poverty.

The Thorsson report led to a 1987 U.N. sponsored International Conference on the Relationship between Disarmament and Development, attended by 150 nations (the U.S. stated that it did not believe in such a relationship and refused to attend). The conference issued a consensus final statement which took a broad approach to security, emphasizing that it consists of "not only military but also political, economic, social, humanitarian and human rights and ecological aspects." Working constructively on all those elements of security, on the one hand, creates conditions conducive to disarmament and, on the other, provides the environment for the successful pursuit of development.

Many countries wanted a special "disarmament fund for development," but the conference, in order to hold Western support, resisted this and instead affirmed an international commitment "to allocate a portion of the resources released through disarmament" to economic and social development in a way that bridges the gap between developed and developing countries. This disarmament dividend – which is still in the future – could be obtained in a variety of ways: trade expansion, technological transfer, reduction of public debt and increased development assistance.

The follow-up to the conference has been very weak, but the document has not lost its importance in putting a global spotlight on the costs of the continuing arms race compared to the benefits of increased development. The conference confirmed the over-arching fact of modern life: global security is a multi-agenda process involving economic and social development as well as arms control measures, the protection of human rights as well as an end to racial discrimination.

The disarmament and development theme was repeated in yet another high-level international study, *Common Security: A Blueprint for Survival.* A 16-member Independent Commission on Disarmament and Security Issues, composed of internationally- known government officials and politicians from Western, Eastern and Third World nations, and headed by Prime Minister Olof Palme of Sweden, proposed in 1982 an extensive list of initiatives to reverse the spiralling arms race and halt the march of governments "toward the brink of a new abyss." As Brandt and Thorsson had done, the Palme Commission emphasized that the increase in military spending threatens the economic security of all countries.

The Palme concept of "common security" stems from one overriding conviction: in the nuclear age, no nation can achieve true security by itself; technology has made the traditional concept of national security obsolete. All nations, rich and poor, peaceful and bellicose, socialist and capitalist, are bound by their vulnerability to attack with nuclear, chemical or biological weapons. Nor are the effects of ecological disaster, economic shifts or information flows confined to any one nation.

> *We are convinced that there would be no victors in nuclear war and that the idea of fighting a limited nuclear war is dangerous. In the nuclear age, states cannot achieve security through competition in arms. They must cooperate to attain the limitations, reduction and eventual abolition of arms. Furthermore, they must develop procedures to resolve conflicts peacefully and stress those modes of national behavior which are consistent with the*

achievement of common security through cooperative methods.

In short, Palme argued that the concept of common security must replace the present policies of deterrence. Nations can only find security in co-operation and not at one other's expense. All states must recognize the legitimacy of the national security imperative of every other nation and, on this basis, work co-operatively to reduce tensions, resolve disputes and reduce armaments. All states are dependent in part upon the restraint of other nations. Force should not be considered except for individual or collective self-defence. Nations should observe more strictly their existing commitments to resolve conflicts by peaceful means.

Common security requires an end to arms competitions through negotiations, national restraint, and a spirit of collective responsibility and mutual confidence. This principle of common security applies to economic as well as to military security. Thus, his report converged on the same understanding of common survival in the global community outlined by Brandt and Thorsson and first expressed by Pearson. Palme drove the point home: "Countries are joined together by economic interdependence as well as by the threat of destruction."

Like its predecessors, the Palme report contains ideas seemingly too big for the political system to absorb – at least, without a prior political determination to try to understand and implement the proposals and education programmes to help the public understand the new route to security. A key Palme proposal to remove battlefield nuclear weapons from a 300-kilometre-wide zone in Central Europe was ignored. Nonetheless, the essence of common security began to take hold in the 1985 superpower summit. The joint communique said Gorbachev and Reagan had "agreed that a nuclear war cannot be won and must never be fought," words taken virtually verbatim from the commission's report. Subsequent steps taken by the superpowers to improve their communications, install systems to prevent accidental war, establish verification systems, and exchange data raised the level of confidence that their relationship could be managed in the interests of greater security.

With the appearance of the Brundtland Report in 1987, the movement for enlarged security picked up some speed. Prime Minister Brundtland made clear that, in the face of global problems of a new magnitude, the world faced a common challenge of a renewed search for multilateral solutions and a restructured international economic system of co-operation. These challenges cut across the divides of national sovereignty, of limited strategies for economic gain and of

separated disciplines of science. Although Olof Palme was assassi-
nated in 1986 on his way home from the cinema in Stockholm, the
Palme commission continued its work and wound up its mandate in
1989 with a final call to humanity not to miss this "historic opportunity. . . to create a radically more peaceful and more humane world."

The final Palme report, like the International Conference on Disarmament and Development, spelled out how security is a broader
and more complex concept than protection from arms and war. The
roots of conflicts and insecurity include poverty, economic disparities
within nations and between them, oppression and the denial of fundamental freedoms. Unless problems of economic and social underdevelopment and ecological damage are addressed, common security
can never be truly attained. Against these threats to humanity's survival, the adversaries in the East-West conflict no longer stand on op-
posite sides; they often confront the same danger, especially in the
North-South divide. Thus, common security could evolve from a concept intended to protect against war to a comprehensive approach to
world peace, social justice, economic development and environmental
protection.

The evolution of an effective and stable international legal and
political framework is essential to meet these goals. Over time, anarchy and power politics must yield to the rule of law among states.
National sovereignty must be respected, but in their own self- interest,
states must learn to exercise collective responsibility and self-restraint,
to cooperate with one another and support the emergence of the rule
of law. Three mutually reinforcing developments are required: First,
nations must resolve, as they undertook to do in signing the U.N.
Charter, to settle conflicts by peaceful means, such as mediation, arbi-
tration and negotiation. Second, international institutions, such as the
International Court of Justice, regional bodies and the subsidiary
agencies of the U.N., must be strengthened. Third, public opinion
must be mobilized, and here non-governmental organizations have a
vital role to play.

Since Washington's and Moscow's choices affect the security and
prosperity of all people, everyone has a right to influence the shape of
the superpowers' arms policies. In the age of interdependence, it is
more than a right: it is a duty. Any serious respect for human dignity
calls for the less militarized societies to play a positive role in bridling
the global war system. A coalition of forces comprising the growing
number of people concerned about the effects of nuclear weapons
could stimulate alternative defence policies for world security en-
hancement.

A number of trends are coinciding to make this a favourable moment to focus on alternatives to deterrence. There is a growing conviction that nuclear diplomacy will never produce a warless world and in a war-prone world some governments may be tempted to use nuclear weapons in combat. Paradoxically, people's confidence that there is no immediate threat of war seems to free them sufficiently of fear to permit a growing support for the shelving of nuclear deterrence, if a relatively unrisky way out of the balance of terror can be found. The time is ripe, maintains Robert Johansen, Senior Fellow, Institute for International Peace Studies at Notre Dame University, to raise three questions.

Why should the U.S. and Soviet Union seek alternatives to nuclear deterrence? First, nuclear deterrence encourages a chronic arms build-up. A war-fighting capability is the logical outcome of an international security system based on competing national armaments and an ever-changing military technology. Second, because of constant maneuvering for technological and deployment advantages in weaponry in order to make the deterrent threat more credible, arms control negotiations are obstructed. Third, nuclear deterrence adds anxieties to crisis decision-making. War may be somewhat less rational than ever, but that does not make war significantly less likely, especially when national security managers emphasize that the key to preventing war is to be willing to fight it. Nuclear deterrence may appear stable in the short run, but in the long run the chances increase of its failing.

How can governments safely move beyond nuclear deterrence? Nations will not give up their arms as long as they rely on them for security. And the risk of nuclear war cannot be substantially reduced without eliminating major conventional war as well. Conventional war cannot be eliminated without reducing the role of military power generally and without protecting nations' security with the aid of international institutions. To move towards a warless world it is necessary to counter the myth that the balance of power system, in its present form, is the only system available to protect security. In short, a security policy capable of moving beyond deterrence must focus on the reduction of military power in world affairs. The inadequacy of military solutions has been vividly illustrated. A world in which there are many centres of political and economic activity will require different approaches. This goal requires broad-based efforts to build global institutions that can enable all societies to be secure. International monitoring and enforcement, economic incentives for demilitarization and international legal procedures would play central roles in replacing deterrence by non-nuclear means.

What immediate steps can be taken to replace nuclear deterrence with a more reliable global security system? On the way to nuclear abolition, a politically viable stop could be made with the establishment of a minimal deterrence system. Robert McNamara, former U.S. Defence Secretary and architect of the "flexible" deterrence strategy, has recently argued in his book, *Blundering Into Disaster*, that a reduction in U.S. and Soviet strategic nuclear warheads to no more than 500 each would produce a stable equilibrium. A similar figure was suggested by the U.S. Center for Defense Information, which concluded that a basic strategic force of 1,000 warheads based on 18 submarines would provide an effective deterrent. The Committee of Soviet Scientists for Peace confirmed that about 600 warheads on land-based mobile missiles would offer the greatest stability in the absence of complete nuclear disarmament. These reductions would be accompanied by the elimination of tactical nuclear weapons and the achievement of parity in conventional forces. Policing an arms agreement that restricts each side to a small number of warheads is quite feasible with present verification technology. While 1,000 nuclear weapons is 1,000 too many, such a radical reduction would have an enormous positive impact on the rest of the world.

Furthermore, both sides could demonstrate their intention to confine themselves to defence by avoiding the deployment of weapons which, by their numbers, design, range, destructive power or geographic location appear to pose an offensive threat to the other. A mutual moratorium on nuclear testing, even for a 12-month period, would not jeopardize current reliability of stocks and would boost mutual confidence. A demilitarized zone in Central Europe, implemented in phased reduction of conventional forces and equipment, would strengthen the security of both East and West.

In all of this, firm foundations for common security would be put in place. These steps would then provide the confidence to move ahead to the withdrawal of superpower armed forces from all Third World countries and establish zones of peace, including the high seas, the Arctic, Antartica, and space.

The Palme Commission holds that the emergence of the rule of law and progress towards the abolition of weapons of mass destruction and conventional disarmament would provide considerable momentum for economic and social development and environmental protection. In the new age, security cannot be said to exist at a personal or national level in a condition of chronic underdevelopment. Poverty itself is insecurity and, actually, far more people in the world today suffer from economic than military insecurity. Cooperation for common security is unlikely in a world where many poor countries face extremely onerous debt burdens, decreasing resources for economic development and widening disparities between rich and poor. Also, international economic insecurity is not solely a matter of concern to poor countries. Serious threats are posed to the whole global economy by trade protectionism, exchange rate instability and lack of effective multilateral economic management. The whole world is affected as poverty spills over from the developing world through enforced migration, various forms of political and religious extremism, the drug trade and AIDS, as well as environmental destruction.

Many obstacles must be surmounted to build this new framework for security. Vision and patience are both needed, for suspicions derived from decades of the Cold War and Third World proxy conflict cannot be erased overnight. A better world with less violence and greater security can be built. A significant step forward has already been taken with the agreement of the 12 member states of the European Community to form a single, fully integrated market in 1992, when goods, people, services and capital will be able to move freely across local borders. The Palme Commission ended its work on this optimistic note: "Common security can be transformed from an idea, a concept, into the common condition of human beings everywhere."

A better spirit of international co-operation ought to lead to structures that continue to build the edifice of common security. No more important task exists than to strengthen the United Nations. A standing U.N. peace-keeping force ought to be at the centre of a revitalized U.N. The Palme Commission foresees enlargement of the present system of monitoring a cease-fire to one in which military units are drawn from member nations for an expanded role of missions mandated by the Security Council which could include: overseeing elections, a task already given to the force sent to Namibia; Maritime peace-keeping in situations such as the conflict in the Persian Gulf, or against piracy and other criminal activity in troubled regions such as Southeast Asia; responding to terrorist incidents and environmental catastrophes; overcoming the disruption of international relief efforts caused by prolonged conflicts within a state.

All this would be financed through a special reserve fund of $2 billion, raised through mandatory contributions assessed to all member states augmented by a levy on arms exports, which would, of course, require the establishment of a U.N. register of private and governmental international arms sales. Of this latter proposal, Secretary-General Perez de Cuellar drily observed: "As long as, regrettably, the arms trade continues, we would at least be robbing war to pay for

peace." The Secretary-General has complained about the present hap-
hazard way of financing peace-keeping forces: "It puts an intolerable
burden on the countries which provide the troops and is also harmful
to the essential principle of collective responsibility."

Although the cost of peace-keeping is infinitesimal compared
with the cost of war, getting governments to pay for peace is still a
major obstacle to common security. This pragmatic reality is doubtless what prevented the Palme Commission from recommending the
logical outcome of an expanded role for peace-keeping: the creation
of a permanent global police force which would consist of individually
recruited persons by the U.N. instead of contingents from national
military forces. Such a force, loyal to the Security Council acting on
behalf of the world community, could not suddenly be crippled by the
threat of unanticipated withdrawal of national units. With no divided
loyalties, a permanent global police force would be a further step in
implementing the international enforcement of rules that must govern
all people. It would augment the present Chapter VII of the U.N. Charter which permits the Security Council to mandate the use of force
against an aggressor. Since Chapter VII is generally unused because of
disagreements within the Council, its intent of stopping conflict would
be upheld by a police force with sufficient moral authority to become
a powerful instrument for co-operation and persuasion.

Other structures for common security are not difficult to envis-
age. We already have the Outer Space Treaty of 1966, which bans
nuclear and other weapons of mass destruction from being placed in
outer space; however, it does not prevent nuclear weapon missiles or
weapons satellites from moving through outer space, the use of space-
based platforms for launching ballistic missiles or the use of satellites
to control and operate nuclear weapons. A World Space Organization
would be a natural complement to the Outer Space Treaty. Such an
agency could ensure that outer space is used to promote disarmament
and development on Earth through the use of satellites under international control to monitor arms control treaties and provide developing
nations with information on flood control and droughts that could
boost food production. An International Disarmament Organization,
responsible to the Security Council, would implement verifiable general disarmament in stages, once nations reach the stage of actually
wanting general disarmament.

The 1982 Law of the Sea Treaty, which the U.N. Secretary- General has called "possibly the most significant legal instrument of this
century," sets out regulations for almost every conceivable aspect of
ocean management ranging from freedom of navigation to the de-

mands of coastal states for proper control of their adjacent waters. In addition, the Law of the Sea provides for equitable benefit from the seabed's untapped mineral wealth now within reach of the high-tech corporations. Despite the enthusiastic support of the great majority of the nations of the world, the Convention has foundered because of the refusal of the United States and some other Western countries to sign it. A more auspicious political climate will be required before the Law of the Sea wins universal support. Similarly, the major Western nations are now opposed to a multilateral verification agency using satellite monitoring systems and on-site inspection, run by the United Nations; they will have to be encouraged, if not pressured, to accept such an authority if disarmament is to be implemented on a global basis.

The Brundtland Commission has laid the groundwork for a U.N. environmental authority, with the power to enforce anti-pollution regulations. This body will be much more easily achieved, largely because of the world-wide awakening to the environmental threat. More problematic, at least in the foreseeable future, is a development authority because the industrialized states show no sign of regulating their trade, finance, resource and technology systems for the benefit of the widest number of people. The closest approximation to a U.N. regulatory body, the United Nations Conference on Trade and Development (UNCTAD), regularly witnesses a debate between the Group of 77 who want a full share in determining the ground rules for raw materials, trade, energy, development and finance and the developed countries who want to keep control of this global agenda. Global economic negotiations are no longer even discussed, let alone acted upon, and it will take a new turn of events – new political personalities, further global economic breakdown – to breathe new fire into the global economic development process.

A legal authority to ban nuclear weapons is also a very distant prospect but not unattainable if sufficient numbers of people, led by legal experts, convince the political order to act. The classical laws of warfare, dating from Hugo Grotius of Holland (1583-1645), the father of international law, have been eclipsed by the totality of nuclear destruction. Until the present era, warfare was at least supposed to have been conducted with limitation and proportionality. To declare nuclear weapons illegal would, of course, run counter to the strategy of deterrence. Nuclear weapons and the core precepts of international law are incompatible. It is illogical to argue that it is forbidden to kill an innocent civilian with a bayonet but that it is legitimate to kill millions of non-combatants with nuclear weapons. Maxwell Cohen, a

Canadian Judge Ad Hoc of the International Court of Justice, has pointed out: "If international law is to retain its ultimate credibility, the international lawyers of the world – everywhere – will have to determine, finally, in common voice the unlawful character of a weapon system that, by serving no policy, and by threatening all values and all life, can achieve no political goal except to assure an end to civilization." An explicit treaty prohibiting the development, manufacture, stockpiling, deployment, or actual use of nuclear weapons would be a major step in ensuring the permanence of common security.

The work of building the structures for common security has barely started. But there is a gathering momentum. Convinced that the present international situation is conducive to their work, some 1,400 representatives of a broad coalition of peace, justice, environmental and world order groups gathered in Washington, D.C. in February, 1989 to develop cooperative strategies. There is an increasing amount of work being done by scholars and organizations, all of which helps to improve the political climate. For example, Marcus Raskin, Distinguished Fellow at the Institute for Policy Studies, Washington, D.C., has prepared a draft treaty for a comprehensive programme for common security and assembled a team of experts to discuss the programme with the leadership of the United States and Soviet Union as well as middle powers.

It is evident that building the structures for common security is an enormous undertaking. Yet not to begin the process, to allow the management of the planet to drift into even more chaos, is to abandon our responsibility to generations yet unborn. The historian Arnold Toynbee once asked: "Will Mankind murder Mother Earth or will he redeem her?" That is the enigmatic question which now confronts us as we race towards a new century.

PART TWO:

Of Nations Large and Small

Chapter 4

The Soviet Union:
Gorbachev at Centre Stage

The meeting was held in the gilded office of Foreign Minister Eduard Shevardnadze inside the Kremlin. Around the table were gathered a team of officials in key political and economic posts in the main centres of the Union of Soviet Socialist Republics. They had come to discuss the progress of *perestroika,* the restructuring program that has become famous throughout the world as the expression of Soviet leader Gorbachev's reforms. The officials reported a general lack of understanding of what Gorbachev was trying to do and, in one case, recalcitrance from a provincial captain. "But you gave him an order!" protested an assistant to Shevardnadze. The Foreign Minister stared out the window. "I know," he said, "but what can we do?"

It is useful to keep this scene in mind as we, outside the Soviet system, watch the Communist Party's struggle to both inspire and control a complete overhaul of the Soviet Union. A strange mixture of elements is being stirred together: a loosening of economic control, labour unrest, nationalist upheaval, political opposition to the Central Committee, resistance to change by local party bosses. The country is in turmoil as it searches for new ways to fulfill the expectations of its citizens now that the lid of repression has been lifted. At the centre of the maelstrom stands its leader, Mikhail Sergeyevich Gorbachev, who has become a spectacular attraction on the world scene.

Born March 2, 1931 in the village of Privolnoe, a farming village in the south of the Russian Republic, Gorbachev is the son and grandson of Communist Party members and became a minor party official after graduation from the Law Department of Moscow State University and the Stavropol Agriculture Institute. In 1978, his provincial reputation, aided by the support of such powerful figures as KGB Chief Yuri Andropov, propelled him into the position of Communist Party Central Committee Secretary in charge of agriculture. In seven years, Leonid Brezhnev, Konstantin Chernenko and Andropov dying in quick succession, Gorbachev became General Secretary at the age of 54.

Almost immediately, he established *glasnost* (openness) as a defining theme to lift the veils of secrecy that had for so long blocked

71

communication between the Soviet Union and the West. This was followed by *perestroika,* a word with many meanings whose essence was described by Gorbachev himself in his book *Perestroika: New Thinking for Our Country and the World:* "Perestroika is a revolution. A decisive acceleration of the socio-economic and cultural development of Soviet society which involves radical changes on the way to a qualitatively new state is undoubtedly a revolutionary task." It is a strange revolution because it comes from the top. Soviet rockets could find Halley's comet and fly to Venus, but household appliances did not work. As Gorbachev put it:

> *An absurd situation was developing. The Soviet Union, the world's biggest producer of steel, raw materials, fuel and energy, has shortfalls in them due to waste or inefficient use. One of the biggest producers of grain for food, it nevertheless has to buy millions of tons of grain a year for fodder. We have the largest number of doctors and hospital beds per thousand of the population and, at the same time, there are glaring shortcomings in our health services.*

Perestroika would intensify the Soviet economy, overcome mass inertia, introduce scientific methods and eliminate the distortions of "socialist ethics." "The essence of *perestroika,*" Gorbachev wrote, "lies in the fact that it unites socialism with democracy and revives the Leninist concept of socialist construction both in theory and in practice." These concepts are scarcely grasped by people abroad any more than they are within the Soviet public, the overwhelming number of whom were born after the 1917 revolution. More tangible was the new law ordering competition among state-owned enterprises, less central control over planning and pricing and more responsibility for local organizations.

However, with stores sparsely stocked with goods and lineups for necessities frequent, the Soviet people cannot yet eat the fruits of *perestroika* and regard dubiously the proposition that they will have to work harder, introduce new techniques and cut through the stagnant bureaucracy before they can indeed eat *perestroika.*

Searching for what he called "Gorbachev's revolution from below," John Battle, of Columbia University's Harriman Institute for Advanced Study of the Soviet Union, reported a lack of evidence that Gorbachev's domestic initiatives were being supported by a large grass-roots movement. "In the fall of 1988, 40 percent of the city's 'esh produce rotted in the train yards because no one unloaded the boxcars. The exhausting daily search for poultry, vegetables, coffee, tea, sugar, wine, vodka and a host of other essential items has left the worker little time to ponder such abstract concepts as democratization." Of 211 standard food products, only 23 were found to be readily available to Moscow consumers.

The skepticism of the public is deep. Decades of broken promises combined with new revelations about the existence of high crime rates, poverty and other social ills have weakened the credibility of the promised reforms. The debate over the nature of reform slows down the process of boosting productivity and, since a large majority of Russians remain unconvinced that reforms will make any real difference in their lives, they are disinclined to put any real effort into the process. A demoralized and confused work force is the end result.

What will help to animate people, however, is the whirlwind of activity called *demokratizatsiya,* a new Soviet form of democracy. Under *demokratizatsiya,* elections in the Soviet Union produced the astounding result of voters voting out many entrenched officials and the rejection by the 542-member Supreme Soviet of several ministers nominated by the Communist Party. The Soviet media has new freedom to concentrate on such topics as food shortages, poor housing, inadequate medical care, drug abuse, prostitution, natural and man-made disasters, and corruption within the bureaucracy.

Although Gorbachev insists that the revolution from above must be accompanied by one from below, in which a revivified people build a dynamic new society, it is by no means certain that this can be achieved. He must do two conflicting things at the same time: de-centralize the economy and institute a profit system with a measure of property and ownership rights while maintaining political control by the Communist Party. He calls this "market socialism," but the hard choices have not been made about where the economic and political lines will be drawn between the security of socialism and the energy of free enterprise.

Democratization, Gorbachev argues, is not only an instrument of reform but an essential element for the enrichment of Soviet society. He allowed the small Baltic states of Lithuania and Estonia (with Latvia right behind) to develop market-oriented economies independent of the central plan that has long governed Soviet business. And he successfully dealt with striking Ukrainian coal miners by accepting their demand for immediate local elections and economic concessions. Yet he dares not completely open up a system that depends for its authority on centralism. Already Soviet conservatives object that the democratization process is undermining the Leninist concept of the authority of the state. Such enterprises as self-financing, private cooperatives and enterprise autonomy, it is argued, challenge sacred tenets of Marxism-Leninism as the ownership of the means of production and the centralisation of economic decision-making. The old-guard bureaucracy see their privileges and perquisites threatened. Yet the mixture of complacency and confusion must be overcome, Soviet Prime Minister Nikolai Ryzhkov has warned.

> *We now need to find new approaches, new methods, new principles to govern relations among the triangle of power that has emerged today in our system of government – the Central Committee, the Supreme Soviet and the USSR Council of Ministers . . . If the party does not find a way out of this then it may lose influence over state government.*

Gorbachev must maintain a critical balance if he is to succeed. On the one hand, he needs a more democratized system to activate the population during the most difficult period of reform. On the other hand, democratization cannot be allowed to threaten the basis of the Soviet system, forcing Gorbachev (or a successor if Gorbachev fails) to crack down and reverse the reform process.

Critical to the maintenance of this balance is the new foreign policy that Gorbachev has developed for the Soviet Union. Gorbachev has become the symbol of hope for a new kind of Soviet Union. And he has intensified the drama by his steady foreign policy moves that led the *New York Times* to declare on April 2, 1989, "The Cold War is over." Considering that the Soviet Union has 11,700 strategic nuclear weapons, more than 10,000 short-range missiles, conducted 17 nuclear tests in 1988 and maintains armed forces numbering 4,258,000 men, the headline was premature. Nonetheless, it and *Time* magazine's assertion that "the Gorbachev revolution has already become one of the greatest dramas and most momentous events of the second half of the 20th century" reflect a growing appreciation in the West of what Gorbachev is trying to do.

The image that has come through to the West is of a more open Soviet society, more concerned about the welfare of its citizens and less with the spread of its ideology and system abroad. A vivid demonstration of openness was the tour of military installations, including a nuclear weapons control centre, provided Admiral William J. Crowe, Chairman of the U.S. Joint Chiefs of Staff, and the highest-ranking American military officer ever to visit the USSR.

Gorbachev has increased openness and self-criticism; initiated significant unilateral disarmament measures; agreed to vastly disproportionate cuts in medium-range missiles; pledged significant unilateral reductions in conventional forces; and, accomplished the Soviet withdrawal from Afghanistan. He has issued exit visas to thousands of Jewish emigres; improved human rights conditions to the extent that the West accepted his proposal for a 1991 international conference on human rights in Moscow; released Andrei Sakharov, the dissident Soviet physicist, from exile and tolerated his public criticism; and allowed the re-opening of Russian churches (the World Council of Churches held a ten-day assembly in Moscow in 1989). Gorbachev openly critized the dictatorial Stalin, saying, "the guilt of Stalin is enormous and unforgivable," and followed that up by engineering the retirement of more than a third of all members of the Central Committee.

On August 6, 1985, the fortieth anniversary of the dropping of the atomic bomb on Hiroshima, Gorbachev announced that the Soviet Union was beginning a unilateral testing moratorium. He maintained it for 18 months, despite the refusal of the U.S. to join in.

With the ongoing moratorium to back up the seriousness of his words, Gorbachev then outlined a comprehensive fifteen-year plan for the elimination of all nuclear weapons. The plan consisted of three phases ending around the year 2000. In phase one, the superpowers would cease testing, remove all medium-range missiles from Europe and reduce their strategic weapons by 50 percent. In phase two, all five nuclear powers would cease testing, and the other three nuclear powers would join the superpowers in reducing their nuclear weapons. In the final stage, all nuclear weapons would be eliminated and a universal accord ensuring they would not be built again would be established. Gorbachev emphasized that the Soviet Union was willing to accept on-site inspection to verify reductions, a willingness he has proven in the INF Treaty. In spite of U.S. reluctance to respond to the plan as a whole, some progress has been made on the first phase. However, if the U.S. continues to resist limits on testing, progress will continue to be desultory.

Star billing awaited the Soviet leader at the United Nations in New York (where Broadway neon lights flashed "Gorby! Gorby!" in welcome). In just over an hour at the General Assembly podium, he gave a sweeping presentation of world reform, the breadth and depth of which stunned delegates. World progress, he said, is only possible through a search for universal human consensus. The principle of freedom of choice is mandatory. The world will find its unity in tolerating diversity. A more intense and open political dialogue is necessary for successful negotiations. One-sided reliance on military power ultimately weakens other components of national security. His renunciation of force won vigourous applause:

> . . . the use or threat of force no longer can or must be an instrument of foreign policy. This applies above all to nuclear arms . . . All of us, and primarily the stronger of us, must exercise self-restraint and totally rule out any outward-oriented use of force.

He then pledged a unilateral reduction of 500,000 Soviet troops, the withdrawal by 1991 of six tank divisions from East Germany, Czechoslovakia, and Hungary, coupled with the reduction in Eastern Europe of 10,000 tanks, 8,500 artillery systems and 800 combat aircraft. Equally striking was his categorical rejection of the world-wide class struggle that was Soviet gospel for so long. "The idea of democratizing the entire world order has become a powerful socio-political force." He called for more political dialogue, "a more intense and open dialogue pointed at the very heart of problems instead of confrontation, at an exchange of constructive ideas instead of recriminations." He linked economic development and protection of the environment with disarmament as the basis for security in the emerging "different world." The commonality of one civilization must become increasingly present in politics. "Perhaps the term perestroika would not be quite appropriate in this context, but I do call for building new international relations."

More of Gorbachev's thinking about security was contained in a 1987 article he published in Pravda and Izvestia, "The Reality and Guarantees of a Secure World." Here he called for a range of new international institutions: a multilateral centre for lessening the dangers of war, an international verification mechanism under U.N. auspices, a tribunal to investigate acts of terrorism, a special fund for humanitarian co-operation, a world space organization, and a "world consultative council of the world's intellectual elite." A central concept was a "system of universal law and order." He set the goal of the dissolution of military blocs, made possible by such steps as the elimination of foreign bases, the creation of chemical weapon and nuclear weapon-free zones and a wider use of peace-keeping forces.

Gorbachev's approach to security is clearly comprehensive. His is a holistic view of the modern world, a high-level articulation of what the Palme and Brundtland commissions have urged. He wants to do away completely with nuclear weapons, put conventional forces into a defensive posture, start military conversion programmes for economic development, strengthen the United Nations system with new international bodies to carry out global strategies, give the International Court of Justice mandatory jurisdiction in a system of universal law and order. The Soviet leader, in short, is advocating global security.

The Soviets Union made formal their ideas for global security in 1986 by submitting a U.N. resolution that sought to establish a "comprehensive system for security." The system envisaged an all-embracing system of international security, encompassing military, political, economic and humanitarian spheres. Many Western and non-aligned states argued that this would be an infringement on the "United Nations system." Although it passed, the resolution deeply divided the General Assembly, which remained divided in a repeat process in 1987. At the 1988 session, the Soviets modified the proposal, calling instead for a dialogue on a "comprehensive approach" to security. This resolution fared better but was still opposed by the United States and its major Western allies (to its credit, Canada voted for the resolution) on the grounds that the diverse elements in a comprehensive approach should be dealt with in their respective forums and committees. The real reason for the hostility to the idea is that it is seen as a move towards a nuclear weapon-free world capable of transforming the political and intellectual identity of the planet. The comprehensive approach to security will require much more analysis, study and dialogue before it enters U.N. strategies, but international political discussion has at least begun.

It is the persistence of Gorbachev's proposals that has impressed his world audience. At first, Western states claimed that he was indulging in propaganda and public relations. While Madison Avenue could doubtless take some lessons from the Soviet leader who pays a lot of attention to his image and specializes in one-upmanship, Gorbachev's commitment to reform is now established. The leading American Sovietologist George Kennan maintains that whoever replaces Gorbachev "would have to follow extensively in his footsteps":

What [the present Soviet leaders] are creating, and what we must now face, is another Russia, entirely identifiable neither with the revolutionary period nor with the centuries of czarist power that preceded it. Just as the designing of this new Russia calls for innovation on the part of those in Moscow who are responsible for it, so it calls for innovation on the part of [the] American government.

It is widely recognized that the West has the most favourable opportunity in the 70 years since the Marxist revolution to develop a constructive relationship with the Soviet Union. The arguments that it was all a Soviet trick or that Gorbachev would quickly be overthrown have been set aside. The challenge to the West to reciprocate in ending the Cold War has now become the central question.

The West has not yet figured out its response. So torn are Western nations with internal debate over "the need to keep our guard up" that significant moves are unlikely for some time. On the occasion of the 40th anniversary of NATO, a seminar of 200 military, political and economic experts was held, producing sharp divisions between those who think that the Soviet Union has entered a new phase of peaceful development and those who fear that the instability of the Soviet economic system will return the country to political oppression. And, in any event, those who argue that it is Western strength that has made Gorbachev react positively (and thus Western military strength must be maintained) still have the upper hand. Peace through strength is an appealing argument that conveniently overlooks the deleterious consequences for the world of continued military build-up.

Gorbachev has demonstrated that at the very heart of his approach is the proposition that the military competition with the West can be moderated and dampened. He has begun the implementation of the cuts in conventional forces that he promised at the U.N., and military spending is to be cut by at least one-third by 1995. He has accepted the principle of asymmetrical reductions in further negotiated cuts. Soviet naval deployments have declined significantly and naval exercises scaled back. In addition, most of the Soviet Union's East European allies have also announced cuts in forces that reduce their contribution to the Warsaw Pact's offensive potential. But as the former chief of the Soviet General Staff, Marshal Sergey Akhromeyev pointed out: "Defensive defence cannot be interpreted one-sidedly, but is contingent on the West and their action."

There are important questions to be answered before it can be determined that the Gorbachev era can actually change the security framework for the world.

Is Soviet Communism evolving into a more permissive state with aspects of democracy, or is Communism decaying and headed for self-destruction?

Will *perestroika* lead to a resurgence of nationalism and uncontrollable uprisings in the non-Russian republics of the USSR and the loss of control in the satellite East European states?

Will the sluggishness of Western response to Gorbachev's proposals for deep arms cuts undermine *perestroika* and require Gorbachev to keep spending up to 20 percent of GNP on defence money desperately needed to meet the economic and social needs of his own people?

Already there are disturbing signs that the difficulties of implementing *perestroika* may prove overpowering and this feeds the arguments of those in the West who caution "wait and see." Dilatory tactics of those still skeptical of the durability of Soviet reforms contribute to the diminishment of Gorbachev's chances for success and by extension to the transformation of international relations to greater security.

It is ironic that the West, whose systems are built on the principle of democracy, has been so slow in recognizing that democratization is the key element of *perestroika*. Though Gorbachev's concept of democracy, one in which elections and free speech are confined to a one-party state, falls short of a Western definition, it is at the heart of the over-arching question: Can Gorbachev succeed?

The demand of some Westerners for the proof of what they consider full reform – multi-party system and the complete marketization of the economy – before they will accept *perestroika* as genuine is not only unrealistic but counter-productive. Gorbachev needs an injection of Western capital, the removal of trade barriers and admittance to international financial institutions to strengthen his financial base. He also needs to cut drastically his military expenses, beyond the 14 percent cut in the defence budget already announced, in order to divert resources into the peacetime economy. Both of these steps require the West's willingness to extend the hand of partnership. A failed Soviet Union is not in Western interests. If the country splinters through economic revolt or nationalist uprising, an unstable leadership might well re-ignite trouble by cracking down on Eastern Europe and reversing reductions in military spending. Western interests are served by a stable Soviet Union, enlarging economic contact with the West and reducing its military forces. In short, the West may not be in a position to make or break *perestroika*, but it most assuredly is in a position to help or hurt Gorbachev's ability to stay in power and advance his reforms, which are good not only for the world economy but for world peace.

The power brokers in the Soviet Union – the Central Committee, the military, the KGB, and the party apparatuses – are watching closely to see whether their man has any real credibility and influence in the West. Business leaders from many countries are rushing to do business in the new Soviet Union, which will strengthen the Soviet economic interchange with the West. But so far, the political leaders in the West have shown little sign of a major response to Gorbachev's proposals for arms reductions, let alone sharing his vision of common security. Actually, the NATO summit of 1989 said, in effect, that the arms race with its increasingly expensive modernization programmes will continue. The West has no intention of pulling back from nuclear deterrence. And it is nuclear deterrence that continues to drive the arms race. Western political leaders have not even begun to face the question of how we can any longer justify the use of a weapon of such magnitude against a country that is struggling to move closer to Western democratic values.

As a minimum meaningful step to respond to Gorbachev's initiatives in a way that would make an impact on the power centres of the Soviet Union, the United States and its allies should pledge no-first-use of nuclear weapons and agree to the negotiated elimination of nuclear weapons in Europe. Proposed Soviet cuts to parity in conventional weapons in Europe make that a politically viable proposal.

Gorbachev needs time for the full weight of his domestic and international proposals to make a lasting imprint on the people of the Soviet Union and the political leaders of the West. Even against skepticism and obstructionism, he has begun the process of transforming every aspect of his nation's political, economic and psychological life. George Kennan, maintaining that Russia under Gorbachev is in many respects the freest period Russia has ever known, told the U.S. Senate Foreign Relations Committee that the time has passed for thinking of the Soviet Union as a military opponent. In his complex and historic circumstances, Gorbachev needs the influence of Western public opinion behind him.

Chapter 5:

The United States: Old Ideals Needed

In 1989, the Bush Administration approved the use of export subsidies on the sale of 1.5 million metric tonnes of wheat to the Soviet Union. The U.S. and the USSR signed an agreement, covering sensitive areas such as laser-weapons testing, radio jamming and accidental incursion of air space, designed to avoid or contain accidental military encounters before they escalate into critical confrontations. Soviet officials visited nuclear power plants in the United States as part of the data exchange programmes of the new World Association of Nuclear Operators, set up after the Chernobyl nuclear accident in the Soviet Union in 1986. At Cape Canaveral, Florida, Soviet scientists participated for the first time in an American planetary mission, the Magellan expedition to Venus, and provided a set of data from their most recent space flight.

The official Moscow-Washington computer link ("hot line") was expanded by a group of American entrepreneurs in a joint venture with the Soviets, who established a two-way satellite connection for the exchange of business and scientific data. Companies from the U.S. and Western Europe rushed with such speed to invest in Soviet industries, ranging from accounting and hotels to copiers and computer software, that 650 joint venture agreements were signed in the first half of 1989, triple the number signed at the end of 1988. In perhaps the most novel arrangement, Pepsico, the soft-drink manufacturer, which has 21 plants in the Soviet Union and wants to open 26 more, purchased from the Soviet government 17 old submarines, a cruiser, a frigate and a destroyer to be resold for scrap as a way of converting rubles into hard currency.

The Kirov Ballet of Leningrad was acclaimed at the Metropolitan Opera House in New York, one of dozens of cultural exchanges between the two countries in which the foremost artists, musicians, dancers and athletes played in each other's country. Academic seminars involving leading intellectual figures of both Eastern and Western nations have become commonplace. Starting with the book *Breakthrough: Emerging New Thinking,* published by the Beyond War

Foundation, Soviet and Western physicists, psychologists, computer scientists, mathematicians and other specialists now regularly publish joint works.

The wide range of exchanges and cooperation by the two governments and a host of non-governmental organizations vividly illustrates the new era in the management of relations between the world's two superpowers. Ahead lie new forms of government-to-government cooperation on fighting pollution, drugs and terrorism, the "transnational issues." The gains made in how each society perceives the other – what the people are like, what their internal problems are, their mutual abhorrence of war – have been instrumental in the building of a new relationship between the two peoples. The television pictures of Ronald Reagan kissing a baby in Red Square and Mikhail Gorbachev clasping hands with throngs on Broadway have reassured the world that Washington and Moscow can get along.

George Bush inherited these favourable winds. He has the opportunity during his presidency to translate the new spirit of cooperation into political, diplomatic and legislative moves that not only respond to Gorbachev's need for disarmament and financial advances but move the world agenda closer to common security. Though Gorbachev's reform has been launched for Soviet interests, many of his proposals are in the interests of the United States, whose deficit problems would be greatly alleviated by major reductions in defence expenditures. Bush has an historic opportunity to slow down and reverse the nuclear arms competition with the Soviet Union. This could be accomplished through a combination of restraint and bilateral arms limitation agreements that prevent the development of new, more dangerous nuclear weapons. The development of the third generation of nuclear weapons, nuclear-driven directed energy weapons, including x-ray lasers, could be shut off by the cessation of all nuclear testing.

The President himself has declared that his goal is bold, more ambitious than any of his predecessors could have thought possible. "The United States now has as its goal much more than simply containing Soviet expansionism. We seek the integration of the Soviet Union into the community of nations. . . Let no one doubt our sincere desire to see *perestoika,* this reform, continue and succeed." Every opportunity will be seized to build a better, more stable relationship with the Soviet Union.

President Bush has offered to cut 30,000 American troops in Europe from the contingent of 305,000 Army and Air Force troops. He has acceded to a Soviet contention that aircraft in Europe be included

in the negotiations for a conventional arms pact. He ordered his negotiators to resume the START negotiations. He stepped up U.S. involvement in seeking a verifiable global ban on chemical weapons. He has
revived the Eisenhower plan for "Open Skies," which would allow
unarmed aircraft from the U.S. and Soviet Union to conduct surveillance flights over the territory of the other country. He has offered to
extend Most Favoured Nation trade status to the Soviet Union.

The Bush Administration takes the view, however, that the na-
tional security of the U.S. and its allies cannot be predicated on hope.
The Soviet Union has promised a more co-operative relationship be-
fore, only to reverse course and return to militarism. Therefore, the
U.S. looks for "enduring, ingrained economic and political change."
"We must not forget that the Soviet Union has acquired awesome mili-
tary capabilities. . . That is a fact of life for me today as President of the
United States," Bush has said.

In this cautionary vein, Bush intends to keep deterrence as central to defence strategy. "In today's world, nuclear forces are essential
to deterrence." ICBM's will be moved out of fixed silos onto mobile
tracks. Production of the Stealth bomber proceeds. Short-range nuclear weapons will be maintained in Europe. SDI will be deployed
when ready. Nuclear testing will continue. By embracing modernization, Bush signals his conviction that it is nuclear weapons that keep
the peace. Though the House and Senate continue to fight over different systems, Congress and the Administration are agreed that a budget of $305 billion is necessary for nuclear arms, conventional
weapons and the race for 21st-century military technology.

The Bush response to Gorbachev's dramatic moves is modest,
designed to show his goodwill while not upsetting the conservative
constituency in the U.S., which is the President's political base. Very
adroit maneuvering is required to hold the support of conservatives,
who are deeply distrustful of the Soviets; maintain the unity of the
Western nations, some of which want to be much more responsive to
Gorbachev; and sustain the East-West rapprochment by concrete
moves. Bush's highly successful visits to Poland and Hungary, where
he boosted the reform process in those countries without, at the same
time, inciting revolt, added to the Administration's goodwill approach.
The U.S. answer to Gorbachev, then, is that the arms race continues –
at least until Gorbachev can prove that he has carried unilateral disarmament to the point where not even the most recalcitrant opponents
of disarmament in the U.S. can claim the Soviet Union is a threat. Gorbachev cannot go that far without significant reciprocal steps along the
way. *Perestroika* needs active disarmament, not just the good wishes,

of the U.S. Administration as the leader of the West. Gorbachev over-came Soviet military opposition to unilateral cuts and, in fact, in preparing for his path-breaking U.N. speech, curtailed the military's role in the policymaking process. Sooner or later, Gorbachev will have to demonstrate to the hard- line element of the Politburo that he is getting something in return. In an unprecedented appearance before the U.S. House Armed Services Committee, Marshal Akhromeyev, now the top military adviser to Gorbachev, warned that significant arms reductions would not be possible as long as the U.S. maintains its position of refusing even to discuss reductions in its overwhelmingly superior naval forces: "When you refuse to negotiate. . . you're merely ignoring the legitimate concerns of the Soviet Union and from there stems the mistrust."

When Bush came to office, he was handed a document called *American Agenda,* a private report prepared before the 1988 election by a high-level team of foreign policy specialists in the Republican and Democratic parties, chaired by former Presidents Gerald Ford and Jimmy Carter. In the section on defence and arms control policy, written by Brent Scowcroft, who became Bush's National Security Adviser, the next President was warned not to neglect strategic offensive force modernization.

Regardless of improved U.S.-Soviet relations and arms control agreements, the Soviet capability to initiate strategic war against the U.S. will persist and a crisis or a political change in the Soviet Union could occur far faster than the U.S. could rebuild neglected strategic forces. Moreover, even with a START agreement, the Soviet ability to threaten all three parts of U.S. strategic forces, as well as their command and control, could continue to improve and U.S. forces will grow relatively more vulnerable over time unless force improvements are made.

Even in the new age of Soviet-American relations, the build-up of nuclear arsenals would be necessary. The potential destruction of U.S. land-based missiles would constantly require ballistic missiles at sea carried by the planned 12 Trident submarines. "They will carry, to be sure, some 2,300 warheads. But this is many eggs in a very few baskets." Without this reserve, the report implied, a START agreement cutting land and air-based nuclear missiles would never be ratified by the Senate. In other words, in order for arms reductions to be approved, arms expansion has to take place.

Similar views were expressed by a blue-ribbon presidential commission containing such names as Henry Kissinger, Zbigniew Brzezinski and William Clark, all former National Security Advisers. Their report, *Discriminate Deterrence,* proposed an "integrated strategy" to enable the U.S. to manage relations among shifting power coalitions expected over the next 20 years. To meet new threats, the commission recommended using high technologies to replace NATO's policy of "flexible response" with "discriminating nuclear responses." Low-yield nuclear weapons, accurately delivered, are commended for future warfare because they would be perceived as causing less than massive damage. Future nuclear weapons would thus be more publicly acceptable than today's brand. New conventional weapons are also needed for the "controlled, discriminate use of force." The commission said that the U.S. military should be prepared for regional interventions in "low-intensity conflict" situations in the developing countries (the Caribbean was mentioned), where insurgencies, terrorism, paramilitary crime, sabotage and other forms of violence occur. Since "low- intensity conflict" has become a permanent form of warfare, new weapons should be invented to fight it, including special communications systems and "smart" (precision-guided) missiles, and the U.S.'s allies in the developing world should be equipped with them.

Given the source of the views in *American Agenda* and *Discriminate Deterrence,* President Bush is unlikely to disregard them, especially since he has not brought to the Presidency articulated views of his own to the contrary. In fact, he has been somewhat skeptical of a vision of a world not dominated by the age-old competition for power. In the balance of power struggles that continue to dominate international relations, Bush does not want to be second.

Other, more moderate, advice has been available to him, however, by a number of prestigious foreign policy associations. The Committee for National Security, a non-profit, non-partisan leadership group formed in 1980 to promote debate on the nature of national security, issued in May 1989, as the Bush Administration was concluding its foreign policy review, a report: *New Thinking in Soviet Defense Policy: New Opportunities for U.S. Arms Control Initiatives.* It recognized that the significant shift in Soviet defence policy towards reducing armaments presented the U.S. with new opportunities for arms control. Gorbachev has seized the momentum in restructuring the East-West security relationship, the Committee noted. "Very large majorities of, for example, West Germans believe that the Soviet Union is no longer a threat to European peace; many even think that the United States presents a greater threat than does the Soviet Union."

The Committee recommended: rapid progress on START negotiations, including submarine-launched cruise missiles and adherence to the strict interpretation of the ABM Treaty, which prevents the testing and deployment of space-based SDI components; the inclusion of ground-attack aircraft in the conventional force negotiations; open negotiations with the Soviet Union on the reduction of short-range nuclear missiles; expansion of confidence-building measures, such as data exchanges with the Soviets; and implementation of a long-range strategy in conventional force reductions by ceasing American expansion in response to Soviet reductions.

President Bush has shown some comfort with this range of policy suggestions which, it will be noted, stop well short of ceasing the arms race. The Committee for National Security says nothing about reviewing deterrence, stopping nuclear testing or preventing modernization of nuclear forces. This latter area is very much the concern of a third source of advice for the President, this one the substantial group of academics, analysts and activists who, throughout the 1980's, have consistently urged the U.S. to get out of the arms race. There is considerable support in the U.S. for such moves as: very large reductions of American troops in Europe; the scaling down of U.S. military bases in Third World countries; the elimination of short-range nuclear weapons in Europe; radical reductions in strategic weapons; an end to nuclear testing (the Democratic Party sketched a CTB policy in its 1988 platform). But these views have not yet become pervasive enough to warrant changes in U.S. policy.

In the melange of viewpoints expressed within the American republic, ranging from the far right to the far left, President Bush has stayed with the familiar. He negotiates arms reductions but he builds new systems. He exercises his leadership in unifying NATO but rejects any modification in NATO's strategy of nuclear deterrence. He proposes American troop cuts in Europe but opposes going beyond a 15-percent cut so that the U.S. does not lose its substantial presence in Europe. He recognizes the astronomical cost of the ambitious SDI programme but advocates a less-expensive model called "brilliant pebbles," whereby the U.S. would litter space with many thousands of small, self-guided missiles designed to track and intercept Soviet ICBMs in flight. He calls for the elimination of barriers to peace but rejects negotiations for a nuclear test ban. The Bush approach is what might be called a traditionalist approach to national security. Speak softly but carry a big stick.

A sharp break from the "traditional" was tried in 1961. President John F. Kennedy and Soviet leader Nikita Khrushchev agreed to authorize their principal arms control negotiators, John M. McCloy and Valerian Zorin, to negotiate a framework for comprehensive disarmament.

In five months, the American and Soviet teams produced a document (known as the McCloy-Zorin principles) which committed the two superpowers to negotiate an agreement to "ensure that disarmament is general and complete and war is no longer an instrument for settling international problems." Arms would be reduced, in a reliable and verifiable way, to the level needed to maintain internal order. In addition, they agreed to "support and provide agreed manpower for a United Nations peace force." The framework document, agreed to by both the U.S. and the Soviet Union, was unanimously endorsed by the U.N. General Assembly. McCloy-Zorin opened the way to mutual acts to end the arms race, but the document was overtaken by the Vietnam War.

A similar opportunity exists for the U.S. and Soviet Union to move forward together to a more secure world. However, Bush advisers and Bush himself hold that a conservative basis for U.S. national security, not idealism, is what is needed to preserve peace. The overall programme for disarmament is rejected in favour of independent negotiations. It is time to move "beyond containment," but not time to move beyond "peace through strength."

This conservative approach is in striking contrast to the radical approach to security offered by Gorbachev. The Soviet leader espouses a comprehensive approach to security achieved through political and legal instruments rather than military force. He wants the abolition of nuclear weapons and deep cuts in conventional forces. The U.S. leader maintains a security policy based on the premise that nuclear weapons must continue to exist and that deterrence is not incompatible with disarmament. Until Soviet reductions and verification commitments are implemented, the West should make no concessions. The Bush approach not only adds to the obstacles Gorbachev must overcome to implement *perestroika* but undermines the U.S. commitment to halt the horizontal spread of nuclear weapons and further complicates the conventional arms negotiations. The gulf between Moscow and Washington is still wide.

Politics, however, is full of compromise. A START accord would at least bring the two leaders closer together (even if it resulted from the lowest common denominator approach, which would doubtless permit continued modernization). Here the help of outside nations, large and small, is important as they encourage and sustain bilateral progress forward by multilateral support. The role of the United Nations in this respect is essential, yet those nations working for stronger multilateralism are often rebuffed by the U.S., whose superpower complex leads it to reject many multilateral solutions to global problems.

The United States refuses to sign the Law of the Sea Treaty, rejects the full jurisdiction of the International Court of Justice and maintains tight control of world financial systems. At the United Nations in 1988, it voted "no" to a multilateral work programme to prepare the way for a CTB, "no" to discussions on keeping outer space free of weapons, "no" to a study of the role of the U.N. in verification, "no" to preliminary work on naval disarmament, "no" to the U.N. undertaking a study of nuclear weapons, "no" to the monitoring of the military application of technological developments, "no" to international cooperation for disarmament through strengthening of the U.N., and "no" to a U.N. report outlining the economic and social consequences of the arms race. In many of those votes, the U.S. stood alone.

The U.S. also voted "no" to the Soviet resolution seeking international dialogue on a comprehensive approach to security. The U.S. Ambassador to the U.N., Vernon Walters, rejected it as a new form of ideology that would replace the present system of pragmatism. "Through its comprehensive approach to international peace and security, the Soviet Union wants to introduce a new system of central control. Defining anything and everything as a 'security' question suggests an ingenuous mechanism by which to control the agenda . . ." The Walters' speech was in sad contrast to President Kennedy's Commencement Address given at American University in Washington, June 10, 1963, which called for a strengthening of the United Nations "to develop it into a genuine world security system" to create the conditions under which arms could finally be abolished:

> *If we cannot end now our differences, at least we can keep make the world safe for diversity. For, in the final analysis, our most basic common link is that we all breathe the same air. We all cherish our children's future. And we are all mortal.*

Having given its agreement in 1978 to the Final Document of the U.N. First Special Session on Disarmament, which listed a Programme of Action intended to be implemented "over the next few years," the U.S. Administration now holds that the Final Document is no longer valid. This policy, denying the work of the international community which had become a foothold for the future, provoked leading Third World countries into escalating demands at the Third Special Session on Disarmament in 1988 with the result that the conference ended in paralysis. As for the U.N. itself, the U.S. government has precipitated a fiscal crisis by not paying its arrears dues, even though the U.N., in response to American pressure, reformed its financial administration.

This rebuff to multilateralism disappoints those who look upon the United States as the leading force for freedom and democracy in the world. It was the U.S. that, through the Marshall Plan, rebuilt Europe following World War II. It was the Peace Corps that sent thousands of volunteers into the villages and *barrios* of the Third World to help people develop their own communities. It was President Kennedy who declared that the U.S. would never negotiate out of fear but never fear to negotiate. The Kennedy assassination, the Vietnam War, the Watergate scandal, the American hostages in Iran, have all sapped the strength from American idealism. The stormy demands in the 1970's of U.N. delegates from Third World countries, unwilling to be passive about six percent of world population in the U.S. consuming 30 percent of world wealth, added to acrimonious relations. A spirit of defensiveness was the dominant characteristic as the 1980's opened. Ronald Reagan vowed to make America No. 1 again.

During his presidency, Reagan, who came to office claiming a "window of vulnerability" existed, spent $2 trillion on defence, the largest peacetime military spending in U.S. history. Spending in the Reagan years on the top ten weapons programmes (B-1 bomber aircraft, F-16 fighter aircraft, Aegis Cruiser, F1A-18 fighter aircraft, MX missile, Seawolf Attack Submarine, Trident II missile, SDI, M-1 Tank, F-15 fighter aircraft) amounted to $167.9 billion. Altogether, some 47 new weapons systems are expected to come off the production line in the next five years. Though the number of non-strategic nuclear warheads declined, the number of strategic weapons increased by 2,500.

The upward defence spending curve levelled off as the result of political pressure to deal with the U.S. deficit. The 1989 defence budget of $305 billion is considerably less than Administration forecasts. Nonetheless, at the end of the Reagan Administration, an impressive number of strategic nuclear weapons systems were being deployed or well along in development: 50 MX missiles installed in Minuteman silos; eight Trident submarines in service; 1,500 air-launched cruise missiles; the B-2 stealth bomber unveiled; the advanced cruise missile (AGM-129) prepared. Spending for these nuclear developments represented only 22.5 percent of the whole defence budget, most of the remainder going for conventional forces in Europe, Asia and the Persian Gulf. The U.S. maintains 375 major bases and hundreds of minor installations in 35 foreign countries. In addition to hundreds of bases in East Germany, Czechoslovakia, Poland, Hungary and Mongolia, the Soviet Union maintains bases in nine countries: Cuba, Syria, Libya, Ethiopia, Angola, South Yemen, Vietnam, the Seychelles and Guinea.

Since 1981, military spending in the U.S. has increased almost three times faster than federal government social and economic spending, and the annual federal budget deficit has grown from $79 billion to $178 billion. To pay for its deficit, the U.S. has borrowed from foreign countries, and in the process has gone from being the world's largest creditor nation to the world's largest debtor. American fiscal policy lies at the heart of current global imbalances. Moreover, military spending has reduced U.S. ability to compete commercially overseas by devoting equipment, materials and skilled workers to military, rather than civilian, production. Government funding for military research now exceeds that for civilian R & D, and the U.S. has fallen below Japan and West Germany in non-military R & D. Two out of every five scientists and engineers in the United States work on an arms-related project. In the past, military technology frequently produced civilian spin-offs, but today's increasingly sophisticated military designs have little adaptability for consumer goods. The main selling point of the B-2 Stealth Bomber, for example, is its radar invisibility, but no civilian airline wants a plane that cannot be seen on radar.

At least 43 states have weapons plants that provide a good living for many thousands of people, and in several states defence is a major industry. Whenever cuts are proposed, politicians always look outside their own states. The local reaction to cuts in defence spending is one of the biggest allies of defence contractors. "What this means," Norman Cousins writes in *The Pathology of Power*, "is that America is allowing itself to become a nation dependent on defence megadollars. . . Ultimately, the danger is not that military spending no longer is the adjunct of foreign policy, but that foreign policy becomes the adjunct of military spending."

The United States Conference of Mayors, concerned about the declining quality of life in the nation's urban centres as a result of funds siphoned off by the military, analyzed the potential impact of a shift in spending. The study found that by diverting to urban programmes only $30 billion for five years from defence (the amount widely held to be wasted by excessive contracts), GNP would rise annually by $3.5 billion, an annual average of 197,500 more jobs would be created, and, as a result of the rise in personal income, federal, state and local tax revenues would increase by $500 million annually. This would be accompanied by substantial improvements in the basic services and public infrastructure in urban areas: more teachers, more housing units, more public transportation, more job training programmes, more help for senior citizens.

The pragmatic argument for shifting some military spending to repair the social deficiencies in the American economy is gathering momentum. When combined with the trade argument that the U.S. is losing its place as a predominant nation and the historical argument that a major shift in international relations is taking place with Gorbachev at the centre of the world drama, the case for getting out of the arms race is immensely strengthened. Even though the seven percent of GNP the U.S. devotes to defence is less than the ten percent under Eisenhower and the nine percent under Kennedy, the U.S. relative share of global production and wealth is only about half what it was then. The trend lines show that as the U.S. continues to devote a disproportionate share of its resources, human and physical, to the arms race, it will be overtaken by those countries, like Japan and West Germany, more dedicated to producing consumer goods than weapons.

The historian Paul Kennedy in his book, *The Rise and Fall of the Great Powers,* points out that the U.S. is now on the horns of an acute dilemma. As a global superpower, it has more extensive military commitments than regional powers like Japan or West Germany and hence requires larger defence forces. Also, since the Soviet Union, even with its 14 percent cut in defence, devotes a greater portion of its GNP to defence, American decision-makers are worried about losing the arms race with Russia. But if the two superpowers continue to allocate huge sums to the unproductive field of armaments, both economies will decline. Gorbachev recognizes this, the U.S. does not.

In the case of the U.S., continued heavy defence spending may so erode commercial competitiveness that the nation will be less secure in the long run. The power and influence the U.S. wielded over world resources in the decades following World War II were wholly out of proportion to its geography, population and natural resources. Now, technological and social-economic change is occurring in the world faster than ever before and the international community is much more politically and culturally diverse. The move from a bipolar to a more multipolar world has clearly begun. The "traditionalists" fear the U.S. will suffer a loss of power and, in their interpretation, will therefore be reduced as the principal defender of freedom in the world. This view, at the very least, underestimates the resilience of the American people. Kennedy concludes:

> *In all of the discussions about the erosion of American leadership, it needs to be repeated again and again that the decline referred to is relative not absolute, and is therefore perfectly natural; and that the only serious threat to the interests of the United States can come from a failure to adjust sensibly to the newer world order.*

As the linchpin of the Western alliance and the centre of the global economy, the U.S. has great responsibilities in the world. The tensions within the republic – within the government itself – are enormous. The fights over policy are often ugly. These pressures defy simple labelling, for they stem from many interpretations of the destiny of the nation. Americans believe they invented the New World in which technology has raised up civilization, and it is, after all, not the Americans who have dominated other nations as the Soviets have in Eastern Europe. They react adversely to attacks on what they think is their fundamental goodness. And they have been attacked by an ever newer world seeking a more equitable division of power. Not realizing how they have hurt others through their competitiveness, they feel aggrieved and distrust that which they cannot control. The movement of the world towards a new form of security requires both trust and verification. The Americans are still between two worlds: the old of confrontation, the new of cooperation. The transition is painful. Trust has not yet been developed. Clamor and confusion are normal.

Yet the innate American energy, so much more powerful than virtually any other country, creates a constant dynamic of motion. Americans are always going some place – in politics, in inventions, in culture. The American astronaut Buzz Aldrin, who walked on the moon with Neil Armstrong, has proposed a new race – a "negotiated nonrace" in partnership with the Soviets – to build a Martian space station. President Bush still sees space exploration as a national venture; the American people, however, increasingly support space missions only as a cooperative U.S.-Soviet exercise. The new possibilities in U.S.-Soviet cooperation could make this planet a safer, more productive and more just home for all.

Chapter 6

Canada: Boldness Required

The 26.1 million people in Canada, 0.5 percent of world population, occupy the second largest country in the world. We are a rich country and the envy of much of the world. Benefitting from the natural resources of the land, minerals, forests and water, Canadians have a GNP per capita income of $18,000, the eighth highest in the world. In any quality of life index – physical, social, economic – Canada stands out. Canada will not be able to preserve (let alone guard) this prime real estate in a world where many developing countries will be literally over-flowing with swollen populations and devastated by environmental catastrophe. Millions upon millions of economic and ecological refugees will demand entry to this haven, which will seem to them a heaven.

The industrial and technological capacity of the country permits Canada to take our place at the seven-nation economic summit. We have not been a colonial power and have few pretensions to grandeur. Our two official founding languages and multiplicity of cultures help us to play a role in the emerging global community. We are identified as a peace-keeping nation (Lester Pearson won the Nobel Peace Prize for Canada's role in originating U.N. peace-keeping), and our involvement in the diverse activities of the U.N. makes Canada the fourth largest contributor to the United Nations system. In the past 20 years, more than 100,000 Canadians have worked on development projects in Third World countries. We were the first country to have the capacity to manufacture nuclear weapons and renounce that ability. As a non-nuclear weapons country, we rid the Canadian Armed Forces of nuclear weapons acquired from our allies.

However, our internationalist tradition, cherished by many Canadians and respected by other countries, has faded in the past decade. This is due to a concentration on internal problems as well as changes in the nature of the international system itself. Renewed East-West tensions in the late 1970's and early 1980's placed a heavy emphasis on bilateral activities, and this was accompanied by declining Western interest in the United Nations process.

Since 1985, a more positive trend has been established and the international climate has shifted accordingly. Once a START accord is

7

35

reached, the nuclear arsenals of the U.K., France and China will be focused on. Already the spread of nuclear and chemical weapons and the global arms trade are receiving more attention. More countries are thinking about ways in which multilateral verification of arms accords can take place, a process that Canada is leading. Most of all, there is a resurgence of interest in using and strengthening the United Nations. All of these changes contribute to an international atmosphere in which Canada can make a substantial and important contribution. An opportunity exists to make the 1990's the decade of global awareness in Canada.

In the long-range interests of preserving and developing Canada as a society where the full potential of people is unrestricted, this country must move with the flow of history. This means a sustained effort to build the structures for global security. Already, the Consultative Group on Disarmament and Arms Control Affairs, a government-sponsored group of 50 Canadians involved in disarmament and strategic issues, has called upon the Canadian government to elaborate a new concept of security, moving beyond the traditional concept in military terms, that can act as a framework for Canadian arms control, disarmament and defence policies. The Group of 78, an informal association of Canadians seeking to promote global priorities for peace and disarmament, argues that Canada should advance the goals of common security through a combined effort with other peoples. "As a middle power . . . Canada carries considerable influence and respect."

The British development economist Barbara Ward argued twenty years ago that middle power states can lead the way in new experiments of cooperation: "The superpowers are too vast, too unwieldy, too locked in their own responsibilities. The great mass of states are too poor and too shaky. It is the middle powers . . . who occupy about the right position on the scale of influence." The Six-Nation Initiative (Argentina, India, Greece, Mexico, Sweden and Tanzania), which pressed the superpowers in 1984 to move towards disarmament, demonstrated the influence that middle-range states can have when they act jointly. The role of middle powers is clearly in the ascendancy. Canada would maximize our influence if we led a group of comparable and like-minded nations comprising the Nordic countries, Australia and New Zealand, and the Netherlands.

Canada, with our history and geography, our freedom and democracy, our resources and technology, our space and industry, is ideally placed to help lead the world towards common security. There is scarcely another country with such an opportunity – and responsibility. Yet Canada has not awakened to the seriousness of world problems and has not discovered how those problems will impact in even stronger ways on Canadians.

Confusion and conflicting messages are in the air. Canada trimmed defence spending in 1989 but stepped up our involvement in the nuclear arms race by allowing the U.S. to test the Advanced Cruise Missile in Canada; one year nuclear-powered submarines were declared vital to our sovereignty and security, the next they were eliminated as too costly. The government supports modernization of nuclear weapons but seeks partial reductions of short-range missiles in Europe; it cut (for the first time ever) official development assistance (ODA) but provided an example for other Western governments in forgiving the ODA debts of the poorest African countries; it tightened restrictions on immigrants and economic refugees but says no political or religious refugees will turned away. Most contradictory of all, defence and ODA, which constitute 14 percent of government spending, absorbed 60 percent of the cuts imposed by the 1989 deficit-cutting budget.

Public opinion polls show that Canadians are concerned about the issues of war and peace, and hunger and poverty, yet the lack of public outcry about the weight of the budget cuts suggest that people are confused about the efficacy of both defence and ODA. Is defence spending of $11.2 billion necessary today? Does $2.7 billion in ODA do anything meaningful to relieve poverty? A sense of direction is missing. Both defence *and* development advocates will be unhappy for the next few years, for the government will not likely reverse its course. There is virtually no constituency for increased defence spending today, and the current government caucus thinks that the present 0.43 percent of GNP in ODA should be the ceiling, not the floor. We Canadians think of ourselves as good world citizens, but there is uncertainty at this time of change about what our principal foreign policy goals should be.

In its combination of wealth, social services and inherent security, Canada is uniquely favoured among nations. Canada has an obligation to the rest of the world to use this fortunate position to analyze the world situation objectively and describe it as it is, without fear or favour. We have no excuse for pandering to the paranoia of worst-case analysts, as occured in the 1987 Defence White Paper. Once Canada recognizes that the role of highly professional armed forces is changing and that they are required less in East-West confrontation in Europe and more as instruments of influence in a broader and more constructive foreign policy that emphasizes a permanent role for peace-keeping, then the nature of the defence debate should change and, with it, the country's readiness to support such investment. Similarly, when Canadians recognize how the economic and social development of the Third World contributes to international security, there will be no countenancing cuts in ODA and the target of 0.7 percent of GNP will finally be met. The shifting of global focus from East-West relations to North-South problems should be emphasized by Canada at this turning point in history.

Canadian political and bureaucratic structures pull us ever closer to the United States at precisely the moment we need to extend our efforts outward into the world community. The political reality is that successive Canadian governments have found their field of action constrained by U.S. policy and the periodic reminder from Washington that the U.S. is the senior defence partner in the Western alliance; that the defence needs of the U.S. require a strong partner along their 9,000-kilometre northern border; that Canada is economically dependent on the U.S.; that Canada needs the active cooperation of the U.S. to clean up the destructive effects of cross-border acid rain; and that Canada benefits from the Defence Production Sharing Agreement between the two countries. That Canada has been able to develop and maintain a distinct foreign policy in the post-war years in the face of this pressure from the south is a tribute to the tenacity of a number of prime ministers (Lester Pearson, John Diefenbaker) and foreign ministers (Howard Green, Paul Martin).

The history of Canada is replete with instances where the right balance between maintaining good bilateral relations with the U.S. and maintaining our own multilateral efforts was a very difficult task. Another such moment is at hand. Canada is on a course leading to increasing integration of the two countries' defence industries. Continental defence programmes have fostered proposals for a common market in defence products. Common defence policies are the object of defence planners in both countries. The Defence White Paper encouraged this activity: "Through participation in Canada-United States Defence Development and Defence Production-Sharing Arrangements, Canada cooperates with the United States in the development and production of defence equipment. . . We will continue to work closely with the United States in an effort to foster the common use of this base."

This excessively close partnership has made Canada unduly dependent on U.S. technology and equipment and the policy decisions that underpin this production. The economic benefits are an illusion and, worse, Canadian dependency deepens an access to a military market buoyed by a relentless arms race. Against this drift to integration, Canada must clearly articulate our own defence and defence production objectives as a primary condition of maintaining our own political and economic independence.

The U.S. pulls us to closer ties in defence and into the East-West balance of power as a very junior "partner." The world needs, instead, our voice and action to strengthen the disarmament, development and environmental bases of global security. Many Canadians seem ready to move in this direction. A 1989 Decima Research poll showed that 60 percent of Canadians oppose Canada and the U.S. adopting identical defence and foreign affairs policies. Similarly, a Gallup Poll showed that 60 percent of Canadians feel our way of life is influenced too much by the U.S.

Canada faces a test of boldness. It will be easier in the short run to stay in the orbit of U.S. activity, which rejects the thesis of common security. But it will be more beneficial in the longer run to recognize the movement of history underway towards ending the arms race, world poverty and environmental degradation through new international partnerships.

This is not just a question of Canadian altruism. It is in the deepest self-interest of the Canada of generations to come to be a vigourous partner in the striking of new coalitions of middle powers of East, West, North and South. Our future trade, our future prosperity, our future stability are all dependant on our influence and involvement in creating the new structures for security that must replace the old dependence on U.S. might premised on nuclear deterrence.

Before Canada can extend a new influence on the changing world, we must first absorb the new security dynamic into our national consciousness and political processes. Canada's defence policy, outlined in the Defence White Paper, has been eviscerated by the Finance Department's deficit-cutting exercise. Its premise, that we must arm against the constant Soviet threat, was outmoded even before publication and was perceived by many Canadians as counter to our foreign policy interests. Similarly, Canada's disarmament policies, which seek disarmament while participating in arms buildups, need revamping at a time when genuine disarmament progress is possible for the first time since World War II. Development, environment and human rights policies all need to be re-examined in the light of the new understanding that security is challenged both by military and non-military threats and that problems of a social, humanitarian, economic and ecological nature demand cooperative solutions.

A new Canadian commitment to achieving global security is essential. This commitment should take the form of a comprehensive policy that harmonizes Canadian efforts with the global strategies advanced by the United Nations. The Pearson, Brandt, Palme and Brundtland reports provide the basis for a new Canadian policy initiative in world affairs. By embarking on such a course, Canada would be signalling that a reformulation of Canadian security policy is a constructive response to the change in East-West relations and the new North-South imperatives. It would indicate a willingness to strengthen international institutions and international law and shift the global security focus from military competition to civil cooperation. A government paper outlining possible policies on common security assigned to a special parliamentary committee would be a major first step. The parliamentary committee should be given a mandate to travel across Canada to receive briefs and hear from Canadians about their expectations of government leadership on global security issues.

A truly bold plan would entail Canada's active involvement in the abolition of all nuclear weapons by all countries, verified by an international institution with the authority to conduct on-site inspection on a universal basis. This would first require Canada's opposition to NATO's modernization of nuclear weapons and an end to the participation in modernization through U.S. cruise missile tests in Canada. It would require Canada to vote for a nuclear freeze in the annual resolutions at the United Nations and to support all resolutions calling for a cessation of nuclear testing.

In the present political climate, these steps do not appear possible, because the Canadian government does not want to break with the United States on security and defence policy. In no field is pressure from the U.S. government as strong as in security. Since Canada sees itself as a team player responsible for alliance unity, and since the government is sensitive to the charge made within NATO that Canada is not carrying its fair share of the defence burden, Canadian leaders are very cautious about not unnecessarily offending the U.S. Administration. Thus the Canadian government tries through a range of multilateral, low-key efforts to advance its arms control and disarmament agenda – always with an eye on the reaction in Washington.

As articulated by the government, there are six basic Canadian arms control and disarmament goals: reductions in strategic nuclear weapons; protection of the Non-Proliferation Treaty; the peaceful use of outer space; a comprehensive nuclear test ban; a ban on chemical and biological weapons; reduction of conventional forces in Europe. Also, much work is being done to improve verification techniques, especially through the use of satellites. Peace-keeping is a vital contribution to the international conflict-resolution process; 80,000 Canadian members of the Armed Forces have served in 16 U.N.-sponsored peace-keeping missions. All of this work, carried out through membership in every multilateral disarmament forum, is a contribution to peace. But, as we have seen, peace today requires more than the traditional efforts that, for the most part, perpetuate the system that guarantees a continuation of the arms race. It is possible, given a sustained demand by the public, for the Canadian government to take responsible initiatives that would contribute to international security without breaking with the U.S. In brief, we can do much more than at present.

Canada must now press for an end to the modernization of nuclear weapons and this position would ally us with West Germany and some smaller European states. Modernization has been the single most important snag in previous arms limitation agreements; it threatens the NPT, obstructs a CTB and heaps fuel on the nuclear arms race. An end to this process is critical to moving away from deterrence and achieving common security. As we have seen, the START agreement, as it is presently being discussed, permits nuclear modernization. Canada should call for immediate negotiations to stop modernization and make clear that it will oppose the deployment of *all* new weapons systems. Without such a firm policy, asserts Ernie Regehr, Project Ploughshares research coordinator, "Canada has little to offer but muted reactions after the fact – which in practice means condemning destabilizing Soviet deployments while 'understanding' American deployments and, ultimately, supporting the latter out of a sense of alliance solidarity."

Opposing modernization would lead, logically, to Canada refusing the U.S. permission to test cruise missile delivery systems here. Canada allows the U.S. to test the air-launched cruise missile (ALCM) over Canadian territory under the Canada-U.S. "Umbrella Test and Evaluation Program." This agreement gave the U.S. the right to test various military systems in Canada, including helicopters, surveillance systems and the guidance system of unarmed air-launched cruise missiles. The Canadian government announced on July 15, 1983 that, as part of the Umbrella Testing Agreement, it would allow the U.S. to test cruise missiles in Canada. The government argued that this would enhance Canada's contribution to the security of NATO and NORAD. Canadian territory was said to be important because areas of Western Canada resemble the geographical structure of territory in the Soviet Union.

The announcement was received with considerable criticism by many Canadians and sparked renewed interest and activity in the

Canadian peace movement. The response was so overwhelming and so negative that then Prime Minister Trudeau felt compelled to respond in the form of an open letter to Canadians. He explained that cruise missile testing would act as a Canadian contribution to the NATO response to the Soviet deployment of SS-20 missiles in the Soviet Union. While some Western European countries were accepting Pershing II and ground-launched cruise missiles (GLCM) on their territory, Canada was allowing four to six cruise missile tests per year over our territory. The U.S. has carried out tests of the ALCM over Canadian territory since 1984.

In January, 1989 the government moved the issue onto a new plane by agreeing to a U.S. request to test the Advanced Cruise Missile (ACM). This decision was taken in secret, with no advance warning to the public, no discussion in caucus, no debate in Parliament. Government spokesmen attempted to explain that the ACM was just an updated model of the ALCM. However, the ACM's much greater range, new materials making it more difficult to detect on radar, and higher accuracy make it a different, more destabilizing weapon than the ALCM.

The USSR is also developing advanced air-launched cruise missiles with radar-evading "stealth" capability and, eventually, with jet engines capable of sustained supersonic flight. This combination of very low detectability and high velocity will produce a significant progressive reduction in warning time, thus blurring the distinction between stabilizing retaliatory weapons and destabilizing, first-strike systems. The development of this weapon should be particularly worrisome to Canada, given the likelihood of an abundance of cruise missiles, of both air and sea-launched variety, capable of striking North American targets. The Canadian government has signed on to the U.S. Air Defence Initiative and this will draw Canada even more closely into U.S. defence plans which will compensate for a reduction of ballistic missiles under a START agreement with increased deployment of cruise missiles.

Banning cruise missile testing would not be a token gesture by Canada but a clear statement that this country will no longer take part in the acceleration of the nuclear arms race. Canada should be urging the superpowers to negotiate a ban on cruise missiles – not abetting their development and, in the words of the Canadian Centre for Arms Control and Disarmament, "starting down a slippery slope in the modernization of cruise missile technology."

A determination to stop modernization should be accompanied by an equal determination to press for a CTB. While the achievement of a CTB is one of the six disarmament goals, Canada has not in recent years fought for it out of deference to the U.S. The government gave only grudging support to the Soviet Union's 18-month moratorium on testing, which the U.S. opposed. And it refuses to support the forthcoming Partial Test Ban Treaty amendment conference, designed to create public pressure for a CTB. This is inconsistent with statements that a CTB is a "fundamental" policy. The argument that confrontation over a CTB could exacerbate multilateral relations is minuscule compared with the great danger ahead for the world if the absence of a CTB results in the downfall of the NPT.

Canada seems content to support the ratification of the Threshold Test Ban Treaty (TTBT) and the Peaceful Nuclear Explosions Treaty (PNET) as a step towards a CTB. But the TTBT threshold of 150 kilotonnes will allow testing to continue unfettered. At the very least, Canada should use the pressure of the PTBT amendment conference to convince the superpowers to amend the TTBT to a two-kilotonne threshold and institute a declining quota of tests over a five-year period. Canada should also press the U.S. not to let the SDI programme undermine the ABM Treaty or hold up strategic arms reductions. And the Canadian government should work for a complete ban on all Anti-Satellite weapons.

As a member of NATO, Canada should press the alliance to adopt a no-first-use of nuclear weapons policy. Reductions in conventional weapons on both sides in Europe, if successful, will remove the concern that has been behind NATO's unwillingness to undertake a no-first use pledge. Canada could also take a leading role in advancing the concept of minimal deterrence.

NATO does not need Canada for our military might (which is slight) but does need our views and voice on multilateral cooperation that can advance East-West *detente*. Some argue that Canada should pull out of NATO, but this would be short-sighted and eliminate our opportunity to influence NATO to become what was envisioned in the 1967 Harmel Report. This report stressed, in addition to deterrence and defence, the need for NATO to pursue a just and lasting peaceful order in Europe. Now that this latter goal is in sight, Canada should be increasing pressure on those within NATO (U.S., U.K., and France) who continue to argue that nuclear weapons are indispensable. This outdated thinking, which is still carrying the day in NATO, is impeding the advance to a new and better kind of security.

When conventional force reductions start to take effect in Europe, Canada should return Canadian forces to Canada. In line with the move to common security, Canada should realign the armed forces to gear them more specifically towards acting as a permanent peace-keeping force as well as fulfilling the basic needs of Canadian security, particularly surveillance of Canadian air space and coastal patrol. Such a posture would be a much more effective and vibrant contribution to peace than the present muted and more-or-less reluctant participation in NATO. And it would help to develop a stronger and more positive relationship between the armed forces and Canadian society and thereby create the basis for public support of adequate and stable defence expenditures. It is erroneous to think that membership in NATO means we have to have Canadian troops permanently stationed in Europe any more than we have to have nuclear weapons. Membership in NATO ought not to demand acquiescence to a war-fighting strategy. Canadian alternative strategies emphasizing the principles of common security should now be heard.

The issue of Canada becoming a nuclear weapon-free zone (NWFZ) will be one of the strongest tests of Canadian boldness in meeting the new challenges, and potential, for global security. More than 180 communities in Canada have declared themselves to be nuclear weapon-free zones. This is a symbolic gesture of rejection of nuclear weapons. The Canadian government, however, does not support declaring Canada a NWFZ. Although Canada does not possess nuclear weapons, NATO does and Canada depends on NATO for our defence. The time has come for Canada to take a step forward.

There are five NWFZs in the world. The Antarctic Treaty of 1959 bans all military activity in the Antarctic. The 1966 Outer Space Treaty bans placing weapons of mass destruction in outer space. The Treaty of Tlatelolco, 1967, established a NWFZ in Latin America. The Sea-Bed Treaty of 1971 bans placing nuclear weapons in the sea-bed. The Treaty of Rarotonga, 1985, created a NWFZ in the South Pacific. Such zones are promoted as confidence and security-building measures. The Palme Report recommended a NWFZ in Central Europe; other NWFZs have been suggested for Northern Europe, Africa and the Middle East.

Another area that ought to be declared a NWFZ is the Arctic and here Canada could play a leading role in mobilizing the support of the Arctic nations. In October 1987 in Murmansk, Gorbachev proposed a zone of peace in the Arctic as a way of reducing East-West tensions. An opportunity now exists for Canada to respond to the Gorbachev proposal. Canada could offer to make the Canadian Arctic a NWFZ and challenge Gorbachev to include the Kola Peninsula, home of Soviet submarines carrying nuclear weapons, as part of Soviet territory to be declared a NWFZ. This would be an important step towards making the whole of Canada a NWFZ, a policy that would result in barring ships carrying nuclear weapons from Canadian ports and prohibiting the manufacture in Canada of components for nuclear weapons. The conditions for the acceptance of this policy, both by NATO and the Canadian public, must be carefully built if U.S. opposition is to be overcome.

Canada's credentials in influencing other nations to pursue the route to common security would be strengthened by adopting forward-minded policies at home. No issue has such domestic political potential as conversion, converting the workforce and industrial base of military spending to the production of goods and services in the civilian sector. Although defence production accounts for less than one percent of Canada's GNP, and only one-half of one percent of Canada's labour force is directly employed in defence industries, the number of Canadians potentially affected by a decline in military spending could mount to several hundred thousand.

When the Canadian government announced the closing of the armed forces base at Summerside, P.E.I., the community erupted in protest against a heavy loss in income. Advance planning based on the recognition that the government has a social obligation to those communities that have come to derive much of their livelihood from defence (as was done when the government closed 17 Pinetree Line radar stations) would have alleviated the Summerside distress.

Although the base, and six others across the country, was closed for financial reasons, the closings led to a realization that disarmament moves can also cost an employee a job. Similarly, the protests by the Innu and other Native peoples against low-level flying by NATO forces in Labrador are brushed aside by the townspeople of Goose Bay who count the economic benefits of the nearby military base. They ardently support Canada's bid to win a new NATO tactical fighter weapons training centre at Goose Bay, even though the number of low-level flights will mushroom. The public demand for economic benefits overcomes any reluctance to see increased military activity in the area.

Peace groups vigourously oppose military expansion and have sometimes prevailed politically, e.g., when the federal government pulled back from bringing a West German arms manufacturer to Cape Breton Island and Litton Systems Canada (which manufactures components for the cruise missile) was kept out of Prince Edward Island. The tug-of-war between disarmament and economic benefits splits communities. The conflict is worse in other countries where defence production and activity occupies a much greater proportion of the GNP.

Lost in the argument are the findings that investments in the civilian economy generate significantly more jobs per dollar spent than investments in the military economy – largely because military industry is so capital intensive. A U.S. Congressional Research study showed that for each $1 billion spent in guided missile production, some 14,000 direct jobs are created; for each $1 billion spent on local transit, 21,500; and for educational services, 63,000. A Canadian study, sponsored by the Canadian Union of Public Employees, showed that in 1983-84, had Canadian military spending been diverted to consumer spending, an additional 111,000 jobs would have been created in Canada. The Lockheed Corporation, a U.S. leader in the aerospace industry, speculated that, instead of weapons, it could practically and profitably move into these areas: space exploration, large-scale construction projects, mining the ocean floor, sea farming, urban development.

Conversion planning is still in its early stages and must be stepped up if the momentum for disarmament is to continue unimpeded. In Sweden, a government-sponsored study recommended that companies in the defence industry set aside a conversion fund each year – two percent of the value of the company's exports of military equipment – which would be allocated for research, development and training for civilian purposes. It also proposed the funding of a "knowledge bank" to assist in converting military industries to civilian production. In the U.S., several drafts of legislation on conversion have been presented to Congress. The most recent, introduced by Congressman Ted Weiss (D-NY) establishes "alternative use committees" at every military facility employing more than 100 persons. These committees are asked to develop detailed plans for converting the plant and reemploying the work force after losing a military contract. A handful of Canadian legislators are preparing similar private members' bills.

The economic effects of disarmament should be viewed in a positive, not negative, light. That is what the 1987 International Conference on the Relationship between Disarmament and Development did in promoting conversion studies. In the consensus final document, nations undertook to consider studies on conversion and publicize the benefits to be derived from reallocation of military resources. Canada was a party to this consensus, but conversion studies have become the victim of policy in which the government extols the economic benefits of military spending. The political climate in Canada is now ready for a major governmental effort to study, plan and explain conversion as a positive step in the disarmament process. More than one seminar or political speech is required, rather a sustained policy that opens up new avenues of action: helping those industries most dependent on Pentagon procurement; reducing Canada's arms exports; assisting local areas to compensate for diminished military income.

The development of conversion plans in Canada would play an important political role in sustaining support for the disarmament process and the search for common security. It would also make Canadians more conscious of the need to improve community life, an attitude that would lead to public support for a stronger Canadian role in boosting global development and environmental protection.

The true purpose of conversion should be kept in mind. It is not just to benefit Canadians in a conflict-prone world but to enable Canadians to play a more effective role in addressing global problems. If military spending in Canada has been motivated in the first place as a Canadian contribution to security and if the definition of security has now changed to embrace the economic and social reasons for regional conflicts, then the Canadian money diverted from defence ought to be channeled to the development needs of the world. In brief, conversion ought to lead to a re-direction of Canadian resources to the promotion of common security.

This is not likely to happen without first overcoming the "aid weariness" that afflicts much of the domestic political and bureaucratic structure. There are, unfortunately, very few votes in aid and that has permitted the government to abandon with impunity the commitment to reach 0.7 percent of GNP in this century. There are several strong reasons for heightened Canadian concern: the moral imperative of alleviating global poverty; the undermining of aid achievements through persistent debt in many countries; the loss of revenue to Canada through lost export sales; the risks to political and environmental security which will prevent the growth of Canada's trading relationships with the developing societies.

Relieving debt in the Third World is a key to future stability. Although Canadian public and private exposure is relatively small, three percent of the amount outstanding, Canada's position within the Economic Seven should be used to argue in favour of the extension of debt relief on a multilateral basis. Moreover, the most powerful governments must be made to see that reducing and eliminating trade barriers are essential to allow developing countries to expand their economies and thus service their debts.

The international system today is lopsided and overburdened. It needs fresh thinking. Canada is instrumentally placed to provide this fresh thinking by breaking out of the stale militaristic mode and developing new coalitions of support to stabilize the world and move it forward. The Canadian government cannot, by itself, stop the arms race, cure world poverty, or protect the global commons but it can – and it must – take more initiatives to solve these problems. Concerned Canadians must push politicians in this direction. A strong and consistent assertion of beliefs and carrying those beliefs into all the councils to which Canada has access would be a positive contribution to energizing the other middle powers to take similar steps. If enough middle powers were willing to work for global security structures, that pressure would produce the accommodations that even superpowers have to make to maintain their international relations.

Chapter 7

India and China:
The Paradoxes Revealed

In March, 1987, the People's Republic of China hosted a U.N. disarmament conference and took evident pride in telling the international audience that the Chinese armed forces had been cut by one million men, 17 military airports and seaports had been opened to civilian use, and the army had planted 250 million trees to improve the environment and help economic development. In the early-morning hours of June 4, 1989, Chinese troops in tanks rolled into Beijing's Tiananmen Square, smashing through tents, and opened fire on student demonstrators, killing, according to Amnesty International, 1000 civilians. The stark contradiction in these two developments reveals yet another impediment to common security: the raw use of power by a government against its own people.

The world was stunned and angered at the Beijing massacre, particularly since the television pictures for days beforehand had shown attractive young people peacefully demonstrating against a repressive regime they said was tired and corrupt. The students wanted at least some elements of democracy introduced and built a replica of the Statue of Liberty in Tiananmen Square to make their point. The Communist government seemed confused at first, particularly since Gorbachev was visiting China on a mission to revive relations between the two countries. The protest continued. But the challenge to authoritarianism went on too long and the government, led by the 84-year-old Deng Xiaoping, struck. The shock waves around the world reflected an immediate sense of outrage. The reaction was deep because people in other lands, watching the events on TV day by day, felt that they almost knew the students. The immediacy of the stream of satellite-transmitted pictures bonded Tiananamen Square with Main Street everywhere. When the students were murdered, it was almost as if it were a death in everyone's family.

But the killing of dissidents in China is nothing new. Amnesty International reports that the Chinese government has executed thousands of people since 1983. Hundreds of thousands were killed in Mao Tsetung's Cultural Revolution, millions in the forced collectivization known as the Great Leap Forward. Since 1949, the Communist dictatorship has been held together by brute force. China's leaders have never shunned the use of violence for political purposes. As former U.S. President Richard Nixon observed, the West has been fascinated by the opening outward of the most populous country in the world, "but China is not Disneyland."

What are the lessons of the abrupt end to the students' struggle for democracy in Tiananmen Square that can be applied to the global search for common security? There are three that bear on the whole international community.

The first lesson is unpalatable for the West but true nonetheless. Democracy is not a precondition for common security. The concept of common security is to guide efforts to eliminate the threat of war between states, on the grounds that modern technology has rendered war obsolete as a means of resolving conflict. All nations, rich or poor, communist or capitalist, democratic or authoritarian, are united in their vulnerability to nuclear attack. All states, even the most powerful, are dependent on the restraint of other nations. The object of common security, then, is not to make the world one in all its ideologies and systems but to make the world safe for diversity.

Such a climate is necessary to allow the natural evolution of human societies. For example, the Chinese students in Tiananmen Square showed in a dramatic way that economic progress without the accompaniment of liberation is not true human development. They needed to be able to participate in setting the conditions for their own destiny. This is a universal characteristic of development, not particular to the Chinese. It is a rising characteristic in all Communist societies today, which is why old-style Communism must give way to new processes of democratization. Common security takes states as they are and its implementation encourages human growth. Democracy, even the one-party kind, may or may not be inevitable; what is evident is the present instability of authoritarian regimes of both left and right.

The second lesson is an emphasis on restraint in the use of force as an instrument of national policy. The blatant use of force, including execution for non-capital offences, is, of course, an obstacle to the building of an international system based on common security. The Chinese leadership must be urged to show restraint in dealing with pro-democracy activists. The hand of the moderates within the Chinese power structure must be strengthened. The moderates lost to an old-guard element in command that did not know how to deal with unrest except in the time-tested way of brutal elimination. The waves of repression, shocking as they were, would have been worse had not public opinion in the West urging restraint been as strong as it was.

It is not true that the Chinese leadership cares nothing for public opinion. In the days following the massacre, clumsy efforts were made to convince people that wholesale shootings *on* the military, rather than *by* the military had taken place. This too reflected the old thinking that power comes from the big lie as well as the barrel of a gun. Deng Xiaoping revealed the vulnerability of China to outside views by emphasizing that the "reform and the open-door policy" would proceed at an even faster pace than before. Having attained his first goal of doubling GNP in his administration, Deng plans to double it again in the next 12 years and, with a two percent annual growth rate, to have China reach the level of a "moderately-developed" country in 50 years. This cannot be done without the infusion of Western technology and this requires a spirit of partnership in development. In the old order, the retention of power by whatever means was given the highest priority. In the new order, which the moderates in China want to build, concern for China's overall relationship with the international community will be increasingly felt. Restraint in the exercise of authoritarianism will have to become a policy.

The third lesson follows from restraint and tolerance. It is not in the interests of security and world peace to have China turn inward and become isolated. Western governments must continue to struggle to find policies which express concern about repression yet do not lead to a break in diplomatic relations. To help the Chinese people without blessing their government requires the delicate touch of moderation and vision. A fundamental goal of Western policy should be to influence the Chinese leadership to proceed with economic reform. This is in the interests of the Chinese people themselves, whose right to economic and social development ought to be a foremost consideration. The amount of influence the West has on China even at times of good relations is always questionable, but to break relations to punish a gerontocracy is to close off influence on future Chinese development.

The Tiananmen Square repression notwithstanding, the Chinese government has shown through its U.N. participation that it wants to play a role in the evolving conditions for international peace. China, which possesses nuclear weapons, is the only developing country with a permanent seat on the Security Council. Each year at the General Assembly, it sponsors resolutions on nuclear and conventional disarmament that win consensus approval. Its policy is to convince the superpowers to cut drastically their nuclear stocks. Only in an international environment of security for all can China complete its internal development. That enduring truth can help overcome the current paradoxes.

Prime Minister Rajiv Ghandi brought the Third U.N. Special Session on Disarmament to life on June 15, 1988 with a programme to eliminate all nuclear weapons by 2010: "Our plan calls upon the international community to negotiate a binding commitment to general and complete disarmament. This commitment must be total. It must be without reservation." Eleven months later, India successfully tested the Agni, its new intermediate-range ballistic missile capable of delivering a nuclear warhead up to 2,500 kilometres. It has acquired from the Soviets a nuclear-powered submarine and its first aircraft carrier is nearing completion. India spends 20 percent of government expenditures on the military and its 1.4 million-member army is the fourth largest in the world after the Soviet Union, China and the U.S. In the 1980's, Indian defence spending more than doubled.

WHICH IS THE REAL INDIA?

The Indian leadership is capable, at one and the same time, of quoting Mahatma Ghandi that "mankind has to get out of violence only through non-violence" and implementing a programme making the country a major military power. The Mahatma, seeking India's independence from Britain, led millions to follow him by fasting, by a willingness to suffer in prison, and by meeting violence with peace. Modern India has sent troops into Sri Lanka and the Maldives, blockaded the landlocked nation of Nepal and has fought three wars with Pakistan. The grandson of Jawaharlal Nehru, India's first Prime Minister and protege of Ghandi, now leads a nation where public opinion polls are 90 percent in favour of the acquisition of nuclear weapons.

Pacifism and guns collided soon after independence in 1947 when India decided it would have to project power in order to be given its rightful place in international affairs. Since the five permanent members of the Security Council brandish their power with nuclear weapons and refuse to stop modernizing them, India reasons that the possession of nuclear weapons is the currency of power in the modern world. It refuses to accept the logic of the major powers that those who possess nuclear weapons are freed of all controls while those without nuclear weapons are policed against their production. The system, Rajiv Ghandi complained to the U.N., "like a whirlpool sucks us into its vortex. We are compelled to divert resources from development to defence to respond to the arsenals which are constructed as a sideshow to great power rivalries."

India, which conducted a nuclear test explosion in 1974, also rationalizes that it acquired the knowledge to make a hydrogen bomb as a hedge against Pakistan's growing atomic ability. If either country tests a nuclear explosive, the other will undoubtedly follow, unleashing a race for increasingly sophisticated nuclear weapons. Although both countries could build and deploy nuclear weapons rapidly, there is no evidence that either has done so. Pakistan has said that it would sign the NPT – if India would also sign. But India resolutely opposes the NPT as long as the nuclear powers continue to test. The NPT, in the Indian view, is a discriminatory document. India wants the NPT replaced with a new treaty outlawing all nuclear weapons. "Corresponding to such a commitment by the nuclear-weapon states," Ghandi said, "those states which are capable of crossing the nuclear weapons threshold must solemnly undertake to restrain themselves."

Thus, India explains the paradox of calling for disarmament and simultaneously arming. To the charge that it employs a double standard, India responds that it is the major powers that have a double standard, pursuing the arms race while attempting to disarm the rest of the world. The onus is on the superpowers to disarm; unless they do, India, along with others in the Third World, will continue to arm. The process of development will be hurt and regional tensions will rise, but the alternative, India reasons, is to perpetuate the division of the world into first-class and second-class states. The Indians have no intention of continuing their second-class status. They see themselves the victims of prejudice. Prime Minister Ghandi said: "History is full of such prejudices paraded as iron laws; that men are superior to women; that white races are superior to the coloured; that colonialism is a civilizing mission; that those who possess nuclear weapons are responsible powers and those who do not are not."

India's population, now at 810 million, will exceed one billion at the turn of the century. Its development problems are immense. There are truly two Indias: the first of perhaps 100 million people who are the participants in, and beneficiaries of, industrial development that has made India a major economic power; the second comprised of the other 700 million who live lives of deprivation. Half of Delhi's 8.2 million residents live below India's poverty line and do without a regular water supply or sewage system. Large families continue to be fostered by low literacy, high infant mortality, inadequate health care and a dearth of information services. Urgent as the control of population is, the government maintains a priority on high-tech military development as the principal way to end second-class status.

India also tries to strengthen its credentials for the disarmament route. It was the first to join the Six-Nation Initiative, sponsored by Parliamentarians Global Action, which pressed the superpowers in 1984 to resume nuclear negotiations and stop nuclear testing. Along with Argentina, Greece, Mexico, Sweden and Tanzania, India appealed to governments, parliaments and citizens to work for common security and peace, and hosted a summit meeting of the Six, who adopted a plan of action in the Delhi Declaration. India is a vigourous participant in the Conference on Disarmament in Geneva and the U.N. discussions on disarmament in New York.

The plan to rid the world of nuclear weapons by 2010, submitted by Ghandi to the U.N., called for progressive steps. First, the INF Treaty must be followed by a 50 percent cut in the strategic arsenals of the superpowers, the cessation of nuclear weapons production and a moratorium on testing. An agreement to forestall the militarization of outer space and international controls to interdict the application of new technologies to military purposes would follow. A single integrated multilateral verification system would ensure that no new nuclear weapons are produced anywhere in the world. Since complete nuclear disarmament depends on conventional reductions, a general reduction of conventional arms across the globe to levels dictated by minimum needs of defence (non-provocative defence) would be instituted. Radical and comprehensive disarmament would accelerate the creation of a new system of comprehensive global security. Such a system would be based on non-violence, respect for various ideologies, the right to pursue different socio-economic systems, and the celebration of diversity.

On the road to common security, the progress and leadership of China and India are crucial because, together, their nearly two billion people are two-fifths of humanity. An analysis of both their situations points to one word as the key to whether they will be willing and able to exercise leadership in building the conditions for common security. The word is restraint.

In smashing the student demonstrators, the Chinese government did not exercise restraint. But that authoritarian use of force has produced such a hostile reaction both inside and outside China that the future conduct of the leadership may reflect a concern for improved standing in the world community. China sees itself as a superpower. Learning self-restraint will be part of that process.

India will not accept the discrimination of being denied nuclear weapons and practices little restraint in its present military programmes. But the superpowers, in their persistent nuclear development, are not showing restraint either. The father of modern India was right, however, in struggling for a non-violent world order. Rajiv Ghandi would serve his own goals better by implementing what the Mahatma taught: "The moral to be legitimately drawn from the supreme tragedy of the bomb is that it will not be destroyed by counter-bombs, even as violence cannot be destroyed by counter-violence." The rest of the world community must be more involved in pressing both – the nuclear weapons powers and the near-nuclears – to practice mutual restraint.

The word restraint sometimes means the deprivation of liberty or the restriction of movement and as such is not an attractive option for a government. But it also means to hold back from doing something in order to effect a form of control. The future security of the planet requires control over the use of force. Common security depends on restraint in the use of authority.

Chapter 8

The United Nations:
The Decline of Military Alliances

The awarding of the 1988 Nobel Peace Prize to the United Nations peace-keeping operations for their "decisive contribution towards the initiation of actual peace negotiations" signalled a new moment of international respect for the U.N. Attacked, undermined and ignored through most of the 1980's, the U.N. has been the victim of the Cold War, political assaults in the name of administrative reform and excessive bureaucracy. Unable to deliver peace and security in the splendid terms of its Charter because the major powers will not let it, the United Nations has been incapacitated by an identity crisis: it is supposed to solve problems that are international in nature, while the authority for dealing with those problems remains vested in nation states. The U.N. struggles to give vision and direction to a world in turmoil and experiencing rapid change without the institutional power to implement its own strategies.

Overtaken by the nuclear explosions of Hiroshima and Nagasaki immediately after its birth, the U.N. suffered the erosion of international idealism that has beset multilateralism the past two decades. The collective security envisioned by the Charter gave way to an assortment of power struggles – with nuclear deterrence at the pinnacle – in which the actions of many nations virtually erased their signature on the Charter. The situation, said Secretary-General Perez de Cuellar, was "partial paralysis."

Yet the U.N. laboured on, its many successes in health, population control, education, agriculture, ecology, technical training and refugee programmes never getting the same intensity of publicity given the confrontations in the General Assembly or the vetoes in the Security Council. It developed peace-keeping missions as a new security mechanism in which soldiers act as a catalyst for peace rather than the instruments of war. Sixteen peace-keeping missions quelled conflicts in the Middle East, Africa and Asia. Peace-keeping principles stemmed from the larger concept of the U.N.'s role in international affairs: impartiality and objectivity, international authority, securing compliance through cooperation, fact-finding, monitoring of agreements, coping with disasters, preventing conflicts. The Nobel Prize has brought back into focus the accomplishments of the U.N. and, more importantly, its potential for a heightened role in building the conditions for security.

The U.N. is coming back into its own at just the moment nations are realizing that the lengthening agenda of security problems is beyond their grasp when acting alone. The major states still jealously guard their sovereignty, but are gradually coming to realize that the U.N. must be brought into the process to supplement their own national efforts. In fact, it was the mediation efforts of the U.N. which resulted in an end to the Iran-Iraq war, the Soviet withdrawal from Afghanistan and the peaceful settlement in Namibia. Perhaps more than at any time in its history, the U.N. is functioning as a truly multilateral institution. Whether these accomplishments represent a genuine renaissance for the U.N. is difficult to assess, but certainly the revitalization of U.N. activity combined with a decline in unilaterally exercised national power point to exciting prospects in the 1990's. That the United Nations, created to end "the scourge of war," is still growing and developing as it approaches its 50th birthday is a sign of hope.

Without a doubt, the United Nations is the key instrument to use to advance the world towards common security. There are many proposals in existence for strengthening, even re-building, the U.N. structure. A rewriting of the Charter is often contemplated by U.N. reformers who would put in a weighted voting system, add a parliamentary wing, conduct direct election of the Assembly members. All this is aimed at helping the U.N. deal effectively in an interdependent world with political and economic problems, with conflict resolution and security. Perhaps conditions in the next century may be ripe for a new Charter, but they are not now. What is needed most of all at this moment is to make the present Charter work. Political energy should be directed not at devising new formulas but at supporting the present strategies for disarmament, development and environmental protection that have been articulated exceedingly well.

Common security will not result from one master plan or the writing of a perfect Charter but from the step-by-step rational integration of diverse approaches to common problems. Common security is not the blossom of a problem-free world; it is the process of collectively assuming responsibility for global security. It is an inherent part of the human condition that there will be disputes between nations just as there are disputes within families. Common security rejects war or coercion as a means of solution. It will become easier to practise when nations, and especially their political and bureaucratic systems, see the world as a single entity.

The present Charter fosters cooperation and the building of a body of international law. Getting on with the business at hand is essential to build the conditions for common security. The agenda for the 1990's contains imperatives for peace and justice, human dignity and freedom that the U.N. can answer, given systematic and coherent action by governments: arresting and reversing the arms race, mediation for the settlement of international disputes, expanding the process of development, achieving universal respect for human rights.

A revitalization of the U.N. involves principally a stronger performance by the Security Council. It can only act when one of the five permanent members does not cast a veto and can only intervene in conflicts between states. The U.N. was criticized for not intervening in the Beijing massacre and preventing the subsequent execution of student protestors. But Article 2, paragraph 7 of the Charter prohibits the U.N. from intervening in matters that are essentially within the domestic jurisdiction of any state – without prejudice to the application of enforcement measures that may be taken in the event of a threat to the peace, breach of the peace or act of aggression. Leaving aside the question of an automatic Chinese veto, it is not clear, under present circumstances, precisely what the U.N. could have done in that one instance.

The U.N. is committed simultaneously to the principles of the maintenance of international peace and security and of non-interference in the internal affairs of states. The balancing of these two principles requires the prudential exercise of diplomacy in determining how the actions of any one state may, in an interdependent world linked not least by nuclear vulnerability, constitute a threat to global security. The Charter allows the Council room to determine what constitutes such a threat, for Article 34 states:

> *The Security Council may investigate any dispute, or any situation which might lead to international friction or give rise to a dispute, in order to determine whether the continuance of the dispute or situation is likely to endanger the maintenance of international peace and security.*

This article has usually been interpreted in a military sense, but today we recognize that non-military threats to security are widespread. Local and regional conflicts have broken out as the result of economic, social and environmental problems as well as military force. The definition of a threat to security has widened and the effect of events in any one country on regional or global peace has widened. An exercise in judgement is called for in any given case.

The Security Council ought to take a wider *tour d'horizon* instead of waiting for disputes to be brought to its attention. This should be done by an annual Council meeting at the summit level. This process would put a world spotlight on all threats to security and build confidence in governments and public alike that the U.N., through the action of heads of government belonging to the Security Council, was involved in protecting security in its fullest sense. An action programme would not come about overnight; but the process of dialogue, of listening to one another, of the human interaction, of the stimulation of officials to produce viable options in addressing problems, of media attention which itself would stimulate public response, of bringing the key people together in one room at regular meetings to formulate a common agenda to deal with interlocking problems that no one nation can solve alone – all this would energize the global political process.

The proposal does not require huge sums of money, structural changes or rewriting the Charter. It requires only the commitment of world leaders to work with one another in a systematic way. Summits have proven their success: the annual Economic Summit of the seven industrial leaders has stimulated the economic expansion of the Western nations and Gorbachev, seeking a link with the Economic Seven, has recognized this value; at the General Assembly of 1985, observing the 40th anniversary of the U.N. many heads of state and heads of government gave their national statements and, while this was not a summit meeting, their presence widened everyone's vision. The 1981 Cancun summit of 22 leaders from North and South at least opened the way to dialogue.

Sustained dialogue at Security Council summits would inevitably lead to proposals for action more in keeping with the nature of modern problems than the measures laid down in Articles 41 and 42 which include sanctions and the use of armed forces. New ideas for the use of current political, economic and social structures for universal benefit would flow in a natural competition of politicians to be seen to be forward-minded. The moral pressure against a state exercising a veto would rise. (Had Council summitry been regularized prior to 1989, it would have been interesting to see the reaction when the Chinese leader met his peers.)

If summitry became a central focus of Council activity, the importance of the Council would grow. To strengthen further its credibility and impact, a slight Charter revision should be made to enlarge the permanent membership to nine from the present five (non-permanent members were expanded from six to ten by Charter amendment in

1965). The four countries to be added should be Brazil, India, Japan and Nigeria. These are nations whose influence and importance has grown enormously since the U.N. began. Such a change would give Latin America and Africa their first entry into permanent membership in the Council and greatly strengthen the participation of Asia. With the U.S., USSR, China, France and the U.K., the four new states would bring to the Council representation of nearly 60 percent of world population. The Security Council would then be much more broadly representative of the modern world and still be kept small enough for efficient business.

Coincident with Security Council summitry, the United Nations could take another step to stabilize world security. That would be the establishment of a "global watch" centre within the U.N. There is at present no central body to assess the risks of conflict arising from economic and social causes as well as political. Recently, the Secretary-General established the Office for Research and Collection of Information, which coordinates analyses carried out by other Secretariat departments. An enlarged mandate would enable a risk reduction centre to recommend to the Secretary-General, and hence to the Security Council, the mobilization and direction of resources to counter a threat to peace. If the resources of the U.N. system as a whole are to be brought to bear in reducing the risk of war and violence, whether in emergency situations or in the longer term, a stronger mechanism for policy direction and programme coordination is required. A "global watch" body, systematically monitoring national and international security developments, could identify overlapping interests and the margins for potential agreement. This would serve one of the U.N.'s principal goals of conflict prevention.

Practical steps in increasing the U.N.'s role in protecting global security are especially timely because of the gradual loosening of military blocs in the East and West. The winding down of the Cold War, concrete disarmament moves by Washington and Moscow and the erosion of mutual threat perceptions provide an opening for the U.N. to play a greater role as the guarantor of security. As world attention shifts away from the old crises of East-West relations to the new development and environment crises of North-South relations, the *raison d' tre* for military alliances will be increasingly challenged. Already, the rigid unity of NATO and the Warsaw Pact is loosening. In the East, Poland and Hungary have staked out democratic lines of action. In the West, the Federal Republic of Germany is leading a move to de-nuclearize Europe, which its NATO partners oppose. The global diffusion of military capabilities will not be sudden; military alliances will not disappear quickly. Indeed, the fight of those opposed to the replacement of the old system of military confrontation with world-wide partnerships for cooperative solutions to global problems will be monumental. But, as East-West tensions continue to decrease and steps towards economic integration are taken, military alliances will not be able to withstand the full momentum of moves to common security.

Just as nuclear deterrence displaced the U.N. collective security system as the means of avoiding war (a change that crippled the U.N.) so now the decline of the militarized means of peacemaking will allow the rebirth of collective security. The need for multilateral approaches to the disarmament agenda is becoming increasingly apparent. The U.N. should be enabled to play a greater role in the development and publication of principles that would be part of a process of confidence-building, better communications and ongoing contact. These are prerequisites to the development of political will to make the Security Council a more authoritative instrument.

The Security Council, which had become almost irrelevant during the Cold War, can reclaim its rightful place as the executive authority in all matters of international security. Forward movement by the U.N. helps to create the very conditions that lead to less reliance on the military alliances. The U.N. must earn the confidence that will lead to its superseding the alliances in importance for security.

Of course, U.N. movement requires the approval, if not the participation, of the five permanent members of the Council. A bit of a vicious circle is created. The way out is to strengthen the leadership hand of the Secretary-General. A new Secretary-General will be elected in 1991. Here again, a candidate is subject to veto before election by the General Assembly. The United Nations Association of the U.S. (UNA-USA) struck an international panel for a two-year study on "The United Nations of Tomorrow" and recommended a single term of seven years (instead of the current repeatable six-year term), which would free the Secretary-General to take more initiatives by removing the need to win approval for renewal. The Secretary-General ought to be in a position to appeal over the heads of governments to the world public.

The UNA-USA panel emphasized the U.N.'s present limitations in the peace and security field are more the product of contemporary international relations than of shortcomings in U.N. management or structure. The U.N. can build on its comparative advantages. The 1980's saw widespread agreement that the U.N. represents the focal point of the international community for fostering multilateral cooperation for peace and security so that bilateral and regional efforts can be complementary and mutually supportive.

The U.N. is structurally placed in a leadership role to advance military security provisions, such as qualitative disarmament, minimal deterrence, peace-keeping, conflict resolution techniques, verification procedures – all steps that would reduce the possibility of war. It is also able to forge a new, non-confrontational way to redirect the vast human and technical resources of the planet from destructive to constructive purposes. Common security does not have a better friend.

PART THREE:

Of People – and You

Chapter 9

Energizing the Political Process

The chances of the political system moving from deterrence to common security are practically nil without the powerful help of outside forces. None of the great movements of our time started at the top of the government pyramid. Not the civil rights, not the political liberation, not the environment, not the women's. They all started with concerned, informed, and committed people working (and suffering) at the local level where they built bases of support that just naturally grew because the time, in each instance, was right. They all built their power from the bottom up, forcing governments to act. So too the peace movement. Physicians, educators, lawyers, scientists, housewives, union members, artists and a range of other disciplines have mobilized to pour into this new international arena their respective viewpoints and competencies. This work has barely started.

The peace movement around the world deserves a substantial share of the credit for some recent government moves, notably the INF Treaty and NATO's agreement to begin negotiations on short-range nuclear weapons when conventional reductions are underway. In Canada, the peace movement vigorously opposed Canadian government involvement in the SDI programme, new weapons manufacturing plants in the Maritimes and the acquisition of nuclear- powered submarines; all of these proposed plans were eventually turned back (the peace movement turned public opinion hostile to the submarines, which the government took into account in cancelling the submarine programme for financial reasons). But, as we have seen, global problems are escalating and the peace movement needs much greater strength in order to make an impact on public policies that can forge the path to common security.

The peace movement is, in fact, at a transition moment of its own. While maintaining its unwavering commitment to disarmament, it must establish new coalitions with development and environmental groups for joint action in advancing common security. This is the biggest challenge the peace movement has ever faced because it must move beyond efforts to stop war onto a much larger and more complex playing field and build the conditions for peace.

When East-West sabre-rattling in the early 1980's alarmed people around the world, the media grew accustomed to measuring the

123

strength of the peace movement by counting the number of marchers. When the INF agreement occurred – when Reagan and Gorbachev began smiling at each other – the resulting easing of tensions seemed to relax the public. Peace movement membership and money fell off. The media and politicians said the peace movement was going away; it no longer registered on the crisis index they use each day to determine what is important. Of course, the peace movement did not go away. Its core membership, recognizing all along that the agreements achieved camouflage the continuation of the arms race, were just as concerned as ever, perhaps more. They recognized that, if public opinion went back to sleep, the lack of continued pressure would allow governments to go back to business as usual, which means seeking disarmament by building up arms.

Protesting such affronts to humanity as continued nuclear testing is still important. But more than protest is needed, especially now that the public has been conditioned to think that there is no need to protest. The long-range impact of the peace movement can only be sustained by developing in the public a consciousness that the combination of global problems must be met by structural reform which lifts up the political, economic and social systems of society to the new levels already demanded by modern technology. Since TV news thrives on action (cameramen love protesters), the peace movement is challenged to find ways of projecting this enlarged approach into media and public consciousness.

The peace movement in Canada enters this new era on a strong foundation. The revitalized movement of the 1980's is a loose network of groups with different aims, philosophies and membership. The unifying factor is that all are deeply concerned by the threat to humankind posed by a spiralling arms race which consumes scarce resources and holds security hostage to ever increasing expenditures. The movement is more broadly based than ever before, including major urban coalitions such as the Toronto Disarmament Network, the Winnipeg Coordinating Committee on Disarmament, End the Arms Race in Vancouver, religious groups such as Project Ploughshares, and organizations of physicians, scientists, educators, lawyers, veterans, artists and athletes. A myriad of local peace groups are established across the country; their membership is both rural and urban and all age groups are represented, with women playing an ever-increasing role.

Many groups come under the umbrella of the Canadian Peace Alliance (CPA). Founded in 1985, the CPA includes 350 individual and umbrella peace groups which represent 1,500 other organizations with peace activities as their primary focus. The CPA has strong ties to organized labour and 20 percent of its members are Canadian Labour Congress affiliates.

One of the largest and most broadly based peace groups in Canada is Project Ploughshares. Established by the Canadian Council of Churches in 1976, it now has 8,000 individual associates from all the major churches throughout Canada. It focuses on three main areas: alternative security, i.e., finding alternative approaches to defence policy and arms control and disarmament; militarism and underdevelopment, in particular military spending and the arms trade in the Third World; and Canadian military production and exports policy. Ploughshares has also developed a national campaign of research, education and publication on the relationship of disarmament and development.

Operation Dismantle, founded in 1977, was particularly active during the late 1970's and early 1980's. Dismantle's main goal at that time was to gain support for a world referendum on disarmament. Today, its main activities are lobbying, public education, co-ordinating campaigns and coalition building directed toward making Canada a nuclear weapon-free zone.

In 1979 a group of Toronto physicians formed a chapter of Canadian Physicians for the Prevention of Nuclear War (CPPNW), linking up with an international medical network which has become a powerful force. The core membership of 7,000 physicians is drawn from across Canada, along with 3,500 nurses, physiotherapists and other health care professionals. Scientists are another group of professionals who are examining peace and security issues more closely and, in particular, the relationship between science and society. Organizations such as Scientists for Peace focus on the arms race and the nuclear threat, while Pugwash and Student Pugwash look at a whole range of global issues from medical ethics and the environment to the arms race and Third World development.

Veterans are another addition to the peace community. Veterans Against Nuclear Arms lobbies politicians and officials in the Departments of National Defence and External Affairs. Lawyers for Social Responsibility reflects the growing concern among middle class professionals about peace and security. The organization encourages and supports legal research on peace, war and disarmament, presents papers with a legal perspective on these issues and provides legal advice to groups and individuals working for peace.

Educators are among the most active participants in the peace movement. One of the most important developments of the 1980's has been the introduction of peace or global education into Canadian schools. Teachers are increasingly pressing school boards to add peace studies and global issues to the curricula.

New research institutes are making an important contribution to the debate on peace and security. The Canadian Institute for International Peace and Security (CIIPS) was created in June 1984 as a crown corporation. Its purpose is to increase knowledge and understanding of the issues related to international peace and security, from a Canadian perspective. It has a budget of $5 million and provides funding and information for groups wishing to promote a discussion of peace and security issues, as well as publishing its own research.

The Canadian Centre for Arms Control and Disarmament (CCACD), established in 1983, is an Ottawa-based private, nonprofit organization which is also doing extensive policy-related research on peace and security issues and disseminates this through an education and information programme. Although it covers all aspects of arms control diplomacy, the Centre tends to focus on issues where Canada is directly involved and where Canadian policy can have a direct impact on the international arms control process.

The Department of External Affairs has also played a role in encouraging the discussion of peace and security issues. The Consultative Group brings together, annually, approximately 50 Canadians to discuss peace and security issues under the chairmanship of the Ambassador for Disarmament. The government's Disarmament Fund has also been an important source of funding for groups or individuals engaged in balanced discussions, research, or publishing of material on disarmament.

To the long list of organizations identified in the public mind as part of the peace movement must now be added the many non-governmental agencies specializing in development and environmental issues. The Canadian Council for International Cooperation, 21 years old, links 120 agencies involved in international development projects; since many of these agencies are sponsored by churches, they represent millions of Canadians. The Canadian International Development Agency (CIDA), the government's development arm, is a principal funder. The North-South Institute, a private group, is leading the way in defining development issues. The Canadian Environmental Network links 1,800 groups across the country (e.g., Pollution Probe, National Survival Institute) working on such issues as wilderness protection, pesticides, waste and energy.

"Peace," "development" and "environment" NGOs have customarily worked in separate streams, but gradually, throughout the extensive NGO community in Canada a better understanding is developing of the complex interrelationship between development, environmental sustainability, the empowerment of women and the poor, and the misallocation of resources to military expenditure. All this work ought to comprise the peace – common security – movement of the 1990's.

NGO activities in Canada have undoubtedly helped to mold public opinion. Many Canadians want their government to take a more active role in disarmament, but they are ambivalent about where Canada's duty, in the interests of security, lies. There is a great deal of discussion about alternative security, the need for international co-operation, and the peaceful resolution of disputes, but in the interim most of the groups have yet to come to terms with combining their principles with a flexible and pragmatic set of strategies for attaining them.

The peace movement is generally treated by government policy-makers as well-meaning but idealistic. The policy-makers are viewed by the peace movement as immersed in technical details that obscure vision and goals. Bridges of communication are obviously called for. But communication itself is insufficient. The peace movement must establish specific, achievable goals, write precise briefs, find their way into ministers' and bureaucrats' offices and convince politicians that it is in their interests to provide political support. That is a tall order. But it must be done to bring the combined weight of concerned people to the democratic process of policy formulation.

The peace movement in the 1990's must combine mature assessments with political effectiveness. Some of this has been tried before, especially during election campaigns, but the 1990's requires a comprehensive approach in Canada to building public pressure for integrated disarmament, development and environment policies. Non-governmental organizations involved in these three fields need to consider the full implications of the final paragraph in Willy Brandt's Introduction to *North-South: A Programme for Survival:*

> *The shaping of our common future is much too important to be left to governments and experts alone. Therefore, our appeal goes to youth, to women's and labour movements, political, intellectual and religious leaders, to scientists and educators, to technicians and managers, to members of the rural and business communities. May they all try to understand and to conduct their affairs in the light of this new challenge.*

The leaders of the disarmament, development and environment groups are instrumentally placed to effect a new coalition for a common security movement in the 1990's that would project their combined strength. By launching a common project, which I have called Project 2000, they could build a grassroots movement that would be an unprecedented political force. The object would be to gather together the leaders of the main groupings of Canadian society, political, religious, business, academic, scientific, agricultural, labour, women and the media, in a huge congress to pledge cooperation in promoting public policies for global security in the third millenium.

Three national conferences would precede this unified gathering. The first, in 1992, would be for leading members of the media, managers and senior journalists, to point out with the help of eminent world leaders the true state of the world today, both the dangers and the opportunities. The second conference, in 1994, would be for the top business leaders, the industrialists and entrepreneurs of Canada, to point out, with expert detail, the mutuality of commercial interests in sustainable development. The third, in 1996, would comprise leading parliamentarians, provincial legislators and mayors and municipal councillors to make political judgements on a societal course of action.

These conferences of three vital sectors of society would prepare a basis of public support for the climactic gathering in 1998 which would be designed to lift up Canadian sights and strategies for the year 2000. Barbara Ward often said that "headstrong" creative thinking is necessary to cope with global problems. Project 2000 is a "headstrong" proposal, calling for a vision and determination to overcome their own rivalries and internal bureaucracies of the non-governmental leaders. But if common security is an amalgam requiring internationally integrated public policies, does it not follow that a unified approach within a country greatly strengthens a government's ability to make a national contribution to the well-being of the global community? The groundwork for an accelerated effort for common security is now being laid by Project Ploughshares, which plans to conduct research, write a manual on common security issues, train volunteers and community peace and justice groups to conduct public education programmes throughout Canada.

Education for global awareness is a precondition for lifting up the national consciousness. In latter years, growing attention has been paid to the role of education in developing in individuals a state of the planet awareness to increase understanding of how global events and conditions shape our daily lives.

The subject of education for peace needs a new, positive perspective if it is to become an important factor in making the world a more secure and equitable home for humanity. Too often peace education is seen, by educators and public alike, in a limited, negative way, as something to counter the fatalism of many young people who fear that a nuclear war will rob them of their future. This is because the full dimension of peace itself is not yet sufficiently appreciated. It is too narrowly seen as the mere absence of war. When common security is properly understood, a new light is thrown on ways to animate and energize a new generation for a global, creative effort unmatched in the history of the world.

The place to start is to examine the United Nations proclamation on the 1986 International Year of Peace. Here the multi-dimensional nature of peace is set out as a global challenge: removal of threats to peace, including the nuclear threat; respect for the principle of non-use of force; resolution of conflicts and peaceful settlement of disputes; confidence-building measures; disarmament; maintenance of outer space for peaceful uses; development; promotion of human rights and fundamental freedoms; de-colonization; elimination of racial discrimination of apartheid; enhancing the quality of life; satisfaction of human needs; protecting the environment.

A wide-ranging programme of education and action is opened up by this definition. Moreover, this approach enables us to comprehend better that peace is established by the implementation of a system of values. Peace demands the attaining of true human security so that people everywhere can live free of the threat of war, free of violations of their human rights, free to develop their own lives to attain economic and social progress. All this is clearly an advance in global thinking. And this advance constitutes a signal of hope to a humanity that has for too long been fractured and frustrated in the attaining of enduring human security.

In short, global education means inculcating in young people an attitude, not only to the world as it is but as it can be. It means helping them understand the magnitude of the transformation occurring in the world. It means opening up their powers of creativity so that they do not just cope with the world but enlarge the community around them. Never has education faced such a challenge.

Global education is thus expanding to include such subjects as peacemaking and non-violence, hunger and the politics of food distribution, ecological balance, international law and organizations, human rights and social justice, world political economy, militarism and the arms race, religious perspectives on justice and peace, culture and community values. There is still in Canada, however, a lamentable lag in using all the vehicles available, the media, NGO programmes and the academic institutions, to develop a sense of world citizenship. A much wider base of public understanding of global realities is necessary to construct a global security system that stands a reasonable chance of political acceptance.

Even though common security is in the interests of all humankind, the obstacles to its implementation should not be under-estimated. Challenging nuclear deterrence will produce a mighty reaction. Fierce opposition will come from a variety of interests, ranging from those who tend to oppose change on principle to those with financial interests in continuing the present system of arms competition. The movement towards common security must be much more sweeping and bolder than just opposing the arms race. It must strike to the root of the problem of national, regional and global insecurities.

The power of this moment of change was eloquently caught by Barbara Ward in her book, *The Home of Man:*

> *In this time of reassessment, in this age of questioning as intense as any since the great debates of the millenium before the birth of Christ, there is a promise of an extraordinary and almost wholly unforeseen fusion of ideas which, separated and even hostile for many centuries, now seem capable of that mutual interpenetration which, in the nuclear as in the intellectual world, can release floods of new energy, new directions, new possibilities, new beings, new forms.*

The modern world faces no less a task than the abolition of war through the establishment of structures that will guarantee equitable and sustainable development of life on the planet. This is no longer a utopian ideal but a pragmatic necessity. The political process will only be fully energized when this idea takes hold. And it is, as we shall now see, a deeply moral concept.

Chapter 10

The Ethical Basis of Change

Science and technology have made evident the integral relationships that dominate the components of modern life. The commonality of life everywhere is thus revealed. The Earth is one place, subdivided, to be sure, into different nations, cultures and ideologies, yet increasingly seen to be perilously fragile or marvelously productive in ways that no one nation or society can control. The roadmap to survival is now clear: political, ideological and economic domination of one group by another must give way to a new range of cultural and societal values to protect the common good of people who stand on "common ground." Pragmatism forces cooperation.

It is through this prism of the power of technology and science, which paradoxically has led the modern world to downplay the authority of religion, that the unity of humankind can be rediscovered. Religion, at its best moments, has emphasized the integral relationship of all human beings. I do not mean merely that there are certain rights every person possesses. Rather, the qualities of intelligence and will provide a wholeness to the person, lifting up each individual as an integral, conscious part of the universe, a reflection of the divine. We have a duty to one another and are even commanded to love one another (an obligation, one would have to say, that is inconsistent with nuclear stockpiling).

It is ironic that the spiritual insight of human unity, lost for so long, is now sharply pointed up by the revelations of technology. The juxtaposition of the spiritual and pragmatic imperatives of "common ground" makes this a fascinating moment in history. From two different streams has emerged the common goal: a better system of sharing stewardship of the planet. The convergence of the two streams – humane values and political realities – creates a powerful flow of thought and makes possible the projection of a new global ethic.

A new global ethic would establish peace as the goal to be reached by enlarging our understanding of security. Security today demands economic and social development, the protection of human rights, an end to discrimination, as well as viable arms control and disarmament steps. We must, in short, increase our understanding and respect for one another as human beings; for we all have the same

joys and sorrows, griefs and hopes. If we can grasp that human recon-
ciliation is at the heart of the new ethic, a new breakthrough to lasting
security can be made. Our common purpose is to live in peace so that
our common home, the planet, can continue to glisten with the glories
of nature and resound with the vibrancy of its inhabitants. This is not
a vague concept, but very precise indeed. Through global cooperation, countries in every region could implement those global strategies for collective security and international economic development
that have been so painstakingly laid out by the United Nations.

On no global problem is there such a pronounced ethical split as
on nuclear deterrence. Those who morally accept and those who
morally reject nuclear deterrence can find supportive arguments for
their position in the extensive literature on the ethics of deterrence. I
hold that the age of *perestroika* demands the ethics of nuclear deterrence be re-addressed, for it ought not to be admissable any longer to
threaten the use of such a totally destructive weapon against a country
that is struggling to move closer to our own democratic values. In this
new era, nuclear deterrence makes a mockery of economic partnerships now developing and distorts the responsibility all peoples share
– who more than in the abundant West? – to build the conditions for
peace defined as global security and sustainable development.

The systemetized acceptance of nuclear deterrence cannot be
expected to change until the moral leaders of society, specifically the
churches, present a unified view to the political order. At present,
spiritual leaders are split. Some even hold that there is no spiritual
solution to deterrence, only a choice among evils. But I hold that
there must be a Christian solution to deterrence. And a Jewish, a Mus-
lim, a Hindu, a Buddhist and all the other religions of the world. What
is religion for if it does not speak with an authoritative moral voice on
the relationship of humanity to God? If it is true that scientists, physicians, lawyers and politicians all failed to take immediate action in
1945 to stop nuclear development and hence avoid deterrence, it is
also true that the voice of religion was muted. That voice has become
stronger but needs to make a greater impact yet. The World Conference on Religion and Peace works to unify the churches, synagogues,
mosques and temples on the great peace themes.

Because of its place in the pantheon of religions, the Catholic
Church has a responsibility to speak clearly and definitively on the
morality of nuclear deterrence. It should, in my view, reassess its present limited toleration of deterrence. Though they elaborated their
concern that a universal public authority be put in place to outlaw war,
the Fathers of the Second Vatican Council, 1962-65, rather grudgingly

accepted the strategy of nuclear deterrence. The accumulation of arms, they said, serves "as a deterrent to possible enemy attack." Thus "peace of a sort" is maintained, though the balance resulting from the arms race threatens to lead to war, not eliminate it. The Catholic position on nuclear deterrence was re-stated by Pope John Paul II in a message to the U.N. Second Special Session on Disarmament:

> *In current conditions, "deterrence" based on balance, certainly not as an end in itself but as a step on the way towards a progressive disarmament, may still be judged morally acceptable. Nonetheless, in order to ensure peace, it is indispensable not to be satisfied with the minimum which is always susceptible to the real danger of explosion.*

In this statement, it is readily seen that deterrence, in order to be acceptable, must lead to disarmament measures. Consequently, deterrence as a single, permanent policy is not acceptable. The American Bishops' *Pastoral Letter on War and Peace,* published in 1983, took up this theme. Though expressing a strong "no" to nuclear war, declaring that a nuclear response to a conventional attack is "morally unjustifiable," and expressing skepticism that any nuclear war could avoid the massive killing of civilians, the bishops gave a "strictly conditioned moral acceptance of nuclear deterrence."

In a five-year follow-up to their letter, the bishops set out criteria to be met in order to continue this morally justifiable basis for deterrence. For example, the bishops said that, in order to be acceptable, nuclear deterrence could not be based on the direct targeting of urban populations. But starting with Hiroshima and Nagasaki, U.S. policy-makers have never excluded the targeting of cities. To destroy the war-making capability of the Soviet Union, the attack cannot exclude the Soviet's valued economic assets, which are located in the industrial-urban complexes. Also, the bishops opposed weapons combining size, accuracy and multiple warheads in a credible first-strike posture. Actually, new weapons now being tested and deployed are enhancing, not lessening, first-strike capability; the modernization process is not just to be able to retaliate against the opponent's strike but to increase the ability to strike first if the need arises.

In Canada, the leaders of the major Christian denominations presented a brief to Prime Minister Trudeau in 1983, rejecting nuclear weapons as a means of deterrence. The leadership of the Catholic Church was a party to this statement, as was again the case in 1988 when the Canadian Council of Churches, sharply critical of the Canadian government's White Paper on Defence, excoriated "the world's obscenely growing stockpile of weapons." Holding that "nuclear deterrence brutalizes friend and foe alike," the Canadian Council this time stopped short of condemnation: "Nuclear deterrence is a judgement on our collective failure to meet our obligation to build peace and justice." This ambiguity was similarly found in the Catholic Bishops' own statement of 1986, which pleaded for disarmament; the bishops did not pronounce themselves on the morality of nuclear deterrence, asserting only that the government "should clarify its own operational understanding of deterrence."

On the other hand, there is no ambiguity in the statements of the World Council of Churches, embracing 300 member churches (but not the Catholic Church) and 400 million people. At its Sixth Assembly, in Vancouver in 1983, the Council declared:

> *The concept of deterrence, the credibility of which depends on the possible use of nuclear weapons, is to be rejected as morally unacceptable and as incapable of safeguarding peace and security in the long term . . . The production and deployment of nuclear weapons as well as their use constitute a crime against humanity . . .*

It is not my purpose here to enlarge upon the divisions that already prevent the ecumenical movement from achieving that unity many desire. But I have cited these official positions, within the Christian family, to illustrate my point that those seeking guidance on the ethics of nuclear deterrence, as the foremost moral-political problem of our time, are left with some ambiguity. The conditions laid down by the Catholic Church, that nuclear deterrence be a step towards disarmament, are not being met. Rather, they are being flaunted, for the NATO statement of the 1989 summit repeatedly emphasized that continuation of the strategy of nuclear deterrence is essential. Even minimal deterrence is resisted by NATO. No thought is being given in NATO councils to moving away from nuclear deterrence because the leaders still deem it inconceivable to live without nuclear weapons. The nuclear strategists have convinced the political leaders that the abolition of nuclear weapons would lead to the capitulation of Western society. We cannot look to political or diplomatic circles to address the future of nuclear deterrence until forced to do so by a public opinion that is led by those who understand the consequences of continued reliance on nuclear deterrence and who recognize that not only is it strategically overtaken by the new Russian revolution but is absolutely morally bankrupt. Gorbachev's *perestroika* has made it no longer possible to argue that it is morally admissible to threaten to blow up the Soviet Union.

This idea will take some time to build and will require the work of peace advocates in all areas. The churches must be in the forefront of this new formulation of public opinion. A united Christian voice, joining with the leaders of other world religions, would be possible if the Catholic Church recognized that, for Western governments, nuclear deterrence is not temporary but a permanent condition and hence no longer qualifies for moral acceptance.

The advances made in re-defining their relationship by Moscow and Washington open the way for a new ethical relationship and the dissolution of the military blocs, something that could not have been foreseen even a few years ago. This past decade especially has revealed the physical, security, economic and social connections that increasingly affect modern life. A new ethical view of nuclear deterrence should come from greater recognition of what the "common ground" of our one planet means. This is by no means confined to church reflection but is the province of all who try to apply the age-old right to live in peace to modern circumstances. The end of nuclear weapons will not leave us with a perfect world but will at least give the political order more room to deal with other imminent threats to peace: the greenhouse effect, world hunger and overpopulation.

Perhaps the very magnitude of the problem will stimulate a new ethic based on re-humanization of the global society. Nothing less than a new ethic can fully respond to the present situation as described by George Kennan in *The Nuclear Delusion:*

> . . . *the readiness to use nuclear weapons against other human beings – against people we do not know, whom we have never seen, and whose guilt or innocence it is not for us to establish – and, in doing so, to place in jeopardy the natural structure upon which all civilization rests, as though the safety and perceived interests of our own generation were more important than everything that has taken place or could take place in civilization: this is nothing less than a presumption, a blasphemy, an indignity – an indignity of monstrous dimensions – offered to God!*

Chapter 11

The Role of Women
in Peace and Development

In ancient Greece, women went on sexual strike until their men stopped fighting. In 1915, the International Suffrage Alliance held a women's Peace conference and out of it came the International League for Peace and Freedom; the League now has 50,000 members in 26 countries and three of its members, Jane Addams, Emily Greene Balch and Alva Myrdal, have won the Nobel Peace Prize. During the 1950's in Canada, the Voice of Women was established to provide organized support for women who wished to challenge the assumptions of the day about military security and the role of women in society; pioneering women, such as Kay MacPherson and Muriel Duckworth, laid the groundwork for a large section of today's peace movement seeking a broader definition of peace as not just arms control but a complete restructuring of society and its priorities.

The involvement of women in the peace issues has a long history. It is estimated that 60 to 70 percent of the peace movement today is made up of women. Yet the role of women in the arms control and disarmament processes of government has been slight. While biology is a poor guide to the approach any given person will take to disarmament, generally women have a more "humane" than "strategic" perspective on foreign policy and their holistic outlook ought to be felt more within government councils. In Canada, there is a move in this direction. As Ambassador for Disarmament, I increased the percentage of women in the government-sponsored Consultative Group on Disarmament and Arms Control from 12 to 43. This does not mean that all the women presented a feminist viewpoint. Far from it; some were more hawkish than the toughest men. Correspondingly, some men I have dealt with are every bit as sensitive and caring about the human condition as women are supposed to be. In government, I have noticed a reluctance by some women to present a feminine viewpoint because they are afraid of being dismissed in the corridors of power. There is, then, no easy categorizing of people in advance by gender. But, on balance, the quest for common security – examining the quality of life as well as the quantity of arms – would be strengthened by greater involvement of women in political, diplomatic and bureaucratic decision-making processes.

The 1982 U.N. Declaration on the Participation of Women in Promoting International Peace and Cooperation is a good benchmark because it makes a connection between women's vital interest in world peace and their right to participate on an equal footing with men in the economic, social, cultural, civil and political affairs of society as a whole. When women representatives of 157 countries gathered in Nairobi in 1985 to mark the U.N. Decade for Women, they emphasized that wars, the arms race and poverty cause constant fear, danger of displacement, physical abuse, social and family destruction and abandonment. Actually, violence is a reality in all women's lives. Throughout the world, women are at risk in their homes, in the streets, and, in some countries, at the hands of the state. Women who suffer violence, being battered, sexually assaulted, harassed or tortured, usually have little recourse. Women are one of the most vulnerable groups in regions affected by armed conflicts. The consensus document *Foward-Looking Strategies* stated:

> *It is evident that women all over the world have manifested their love for peace and their wish to play a greater role in international cooperation, amity and peace among different nations. All obstacles at national and international levels in the way of women's participation in promoting international peace and cooperation should be removed as soon as possible.*

The wide scope of *Forward-Looking Strategies* has added to the momentum not only of the quest for women's rights but participation of women in the common security issues. There is a long way to go before there is equal representation, but the Western governments are becoming more sensitive to the need to weave into the political processes the distinctive approach to peace and development that women are capable of bringing.

Whether this gradual opening to women will result in a shift from competition and confrontation to more cooperation remains to be seen. It has frequently been the case that women who entered the system were changed by the system and thus have only marginal effect on it. For this reason, many women choose to stay outside the inner circles of government and direct their energy instead to changing the underlying structures of society that promote militarism in international relations. Those women who choose to educate, lobby and otherwise work as peace activists deserve respect and support, for they are are filling a vital function. The new *Directory of Canadian Women Specializing in Global Issues,* published by the Canadian Council for International Cooperation, reveals the large number of highly qualified women in community groups, schools, universities, churches, labour unions and urban centres playing important roles in the social justice issues.

In developed as well as in developing societies, women are discriminated against. The demand for equal pay for work of equal value runs up against the barriers of costs and profits. Women's struggle for quality and affordable day care is impeded by societal norms that do not give sufficient priority to the well-being of children or the responsibilities of motherhood. Since women now participate so fully in the workforce, employers should offer child care services to workers and governments should offer incentives to employers to provide these services. Women are at the heart of development everywhere, and the pursuit of global security would be advanced by helping women cope with their everyday responsibilities.

In developing countries, women are stuck with most of the non-money economy (subsistence agriculture, bearing and raising children, domestic labour) and take an important part in the money economy (trading, wage employment). Much of this work is unrecognized and those who do it receive little support. Their health suffers, their work suffers, their children suffer. Just to transport water, fuel and goods between home and market, women work the equivalent of an eight-hour job. They are left to provide more of the basic health care, education and nursing of the young and elderly because most Third World governments cut back what meagre services they did provide in the debt-ridden 1980's. Development itself is held back as a result.

The costs are high in ignoring the needs of women: uncontrolled population growth, high infant and child mortality, low literacy, a weakened economy, ineffective agriculture, a deteriorating environment. For girls and young women it means unequal opportunities, a higher level of risk and a life pre-determined by fate and the decisions of others rather than their own choice. Investing in women means widening their choice of strategies and reducing their dependence on children for status and support. Family planning is one of the most important investments, but other "social investments," health and education, are equally important. Investment in women must go beyond services and remove the barriers preventing them from exploring their full potential. That means granting them equal access to land, to credit, to rewarding employment as well as establishing their personal and political rights. Dr. Nafis Sadik, executive director of the United Nations Population Fund, has put the problem and the challenge succinctly:

> *. . . The extent to which women are free to make decisions affecting their lives may be the key to the future, not only of the poor countries but of the richer ones too. As mothers, producers or suppliers of food, fuel and water, trades and manufacturers, political and community leaders, women are at the centre of the process of change.*

Sustainable development can only be achieved with the full and equal participation of women; when population, environmental and development linkages are adequately translated into policies and programmes and when social needs are given equal priority with economic growth. The immediate priorities are: documenting and publicizing women's vital contribution to development; increasing the productivity of women and lessening their double burden; providing family planning services; improving the health of women; expanding education; ensuring equality of opportunity. The U.N. has put a spotlight on women's priorities with a new agency, United Nations Development Fund for Women (UNIFEM), which provides financial and technical support to poor Third World women involved in cooperative activities, food production, fuel and water supply, health services and small businesses. It is directed by a Canadian, Sharon Capeling-Alakija, a development specialist who believes women can be the agents for meaningful development in the future if their productivity is increased by technology and training and if the burden they carry in time-consuming chores can be lessened. UNIFEM's $40-million budget is tiny compared to the need, and scandalouly deficient compared to the money spend on arms. But it is a catalyst for change.

There must now be a strengthening of all women's programmes throughout the U.N. system and the enlargement of regional institutes to promote more activity by women in peace and development issues. Governments should facilitate women's active participation in the decision-making processes related to international peace and development; strengthen the role of women in educating and promoting peace and cooperation; remove discriminatory practices against women in the workplace; provide equal opportunities for women to participate in programmes to upgrade the environment; and provide health and social services to meet the needs of the most vulnerable groups in society.

The role of women in peace and development is to dislodge the old assumptions, to bring a more humane perspective to issues, to overcome the militarist thinking that has led to so much deprivation. By seeing peace through the economic and social needs of women throughout the world, the enormous and often abstract problems of achieving global security are placed in a more manageable setting.

Chapter 12

45 Things You Can Do For Peace

Peace is a public matter. But it is also personal. Every inhabitant of the planet is affected by the search for global security. And every inhabitant can affect that search. Peace is not just the responsibility of the Secretary-General of the United Nations. It is your responsibility, too. Peace is inter-personal and multi-dimensional. It is foremost attitudinal. There is no end to what you can do for peace with security and social justice for all. Learn, use your influence, generate community action. Here is a list of 45 things, for a start, that you can do.

1. Pin a photograph of Earth as seen from outer space on your kitchen bulletin board. The oneness of the planet is a source of continuing inspiration. Full-size colour posters are available for $4 from World Federalists of Canada, 145 Spruce Street, Suite 207, Ottawa, Ontario K1R 6P1.
2. Do whatever you are good at. A group of women in Saskatchewan knitted a "peace quilt" and sent it to the Canadian Mission to the United Nations; it now hangs in the Mission conference room and has favourably impressed diplomats who regularly attend disarmament meetings there.
3. Read the Brundtland Report and find out what "sustainable development" is all about. It is called *Our Common Future* (Oxford University Press), and is available in bookstores.
4. Become an "ecological citizen." Knowing the Earth faces ecological catastrophe is only the beginning. A sense of urgency must be developed by everyone. The place to start is at home. Recycle paper and glass products. Support a garbage tax on non-recyclable material. Learn which products use chlorofluorocarbons (CFCs) and avoid them.
5. Look for industries in your community that pollute. Draw the attention of the community to this. Learn how industrialized societies are dumping toxic wastes in Third World countries. Support raising fuel standards for vehicles. Fight to keep train service. Support mass transit.
6. Plant a tree. Trees have traditionally been planted in commemoration of loved ones. They feature in all the world's religions as

a symbolic union of the forces of the Earth with those of the heavens. Also, trees are essential to the biosphere, and the American Forestry Association, a citizens' conservation organization, has undertaken a campaign aimed at planting 100 million new trees by 1992 to ease the threat of global warming.

7. Ask your teen-age children to invite their friends to a showing of "Mile Zero: The Safe Tour," a 48-minute NFB film about four young Canadians who carried their message of global peace and disarmament across Canada. Available for purchase or rental from National Film Board of Canada, P.O. Box 6100, Station A, Montreal, Quebec H3C 3H5.

8. Join a non-governmental organization in your community: Project Ploughshares, United Nations Association in Canada, Development and Peace are just a few of the national organizations that have local branches across the country.

9. Order the Canadian Peace Directory, an annotated guide to more than 520 peace organizations, catalogued by geography, group type and specific issues. Available for $5 from Canadian Peace Alliance, 555 Bloor Street W., Toronto, Ontario, M5S 1Y6, (416) 588-5555. Find a congenial group and support it.

10. Soviet and other East European visitors to Canada are now becoming common as athletic, scientific, educational and cultural exchanges multiply. Find out from local authorities when visitors are coming and invite someone to your home for dinner. The same applies to visitors from Third World countries.

11. Ask your municipality to fly the United Nations flag all year long. Many do. Work to have a municipal peace park or garden. Follow Toronto City Council's example and have your municipality establish a Peace Committee. More than 180 municipalities in Canada have declared themselves a nuclear weapon-free zone. Has yours?

12. In Canada, the twinning of cities and towns with counterparts in other parts of the world is a well-established practice. Is your municipality twinned? The Federation of Canadian Municipalities, 24 Clarence Street, Ottawa, Ontario, K1N 5P3, (613) 237-5221 will provide information on how to twin with a Soviet or other East European municipality.

13. With a group of friends or in a local organization, form a "media watch" to monitor what press, radio and TV are reporting on the issue of disarmament, development and the environment. Compliment the editor or producer when a good report (even if it's of bad news) appears. Complain if you feel that in-depth treatment to serious issues is not being given.

14. Invite a representative of your local paper or TV station to your group's meeting for the purpose of a dialogue about the media treatment of global problems and what your group might do to keep the media informed.

15. If you are interviewed by the media, remember that the interviewer is seeking controversy. Confrontational stances are encouraged. But that's not a very effective way for you to get across a positive message. Stay on your agenda. This takes practice.

16. The communication of your views in a way that contributes to consciousness-raising in your community is one of the most important things you can do. Start by gently turning the conversation upward over coffee or lunch at work. Most people are afraid of being seen as preaching, but it isn't preaching to comment on nuclear disarmament talks, a famine in Africa, the burning of forests in Brazil, or the pollution of the St. Lawrence River.

17. Letters to the editor, preferably short, well-reasoned, and devoid of sarcasm, are an excellent way of sharpening a community's focus on a subject.

18. The secretaries of M.P.s (and provincial legislators) have form letters on almost any subject ready for response to your letter. Your next move is to write a second letter to the M.P., picking up on a point in his or her (form) letter. There is no form answer to a second letter. The M.P. has to read it in order to respond. In the process, if your letter is, to repeat, short, well-reasoned and devoid of sarcasm, the M.P. will probably learn from you.

19. A visit to an M.P. is even better than a letter. No M.P. will refuse your request for an appointment in the constituency office. A delegation from your group (three or four maximum) should bring a prepared statement or short brief on the subject you want to discuss. Get your facts right. Know the M.P.'s (or the party's) position beforehand. State your case politely and with the assurance that you know what you're talking about. Don't harrangue the M.P. Don't piggy-back other issues on to the main purpose of the visit. Don't overstay your appointment time.

20. Even if your M.P. is favourably disposed to your viewpoint, his or her influence in caucus and in Parliament is probably much less than you imagine. You have to go beyond the M.P. A very effective, and under-utilized, way to connect with the political process is to send your statement or brief also to the chairman

of the appropriate parliamentary committee, e.g. External Affairs, Defence, Environment, etc. The membership of these committees is listed at the back of Hansard each Wednesday. The minutes of their meetings are available by writing to the secretary of the designated committee (c/o House of Commons, Ottawa, Ontario, K1A 0A6) Write to the Chairman and send a copy to each member of the committee. The steering committee, composed of members of all parties, is bound to notice your communication.

21. How did your M.P. get into office? Ordinarily, by being nominated by a political party. Who nominates the candidate? Ordinarily, a handful of people who organize supporters to come to the nomination meeting. If you know someone (maybe even you) who represents your beliefs, why not organize that person's candidacy? Grass-roots organization is what democracy is all about. It won't be easy, but you'll meet all manner of people in your community and be a better person for the process.

22. Even if you're not one of the organizers, go to nomination meetings and get to know the candidates. Attend all-candidate election forums and try to get candidates to state their views on issues important to you. Work for the candidate who will *do* something. Follow up after the election.

23. Once your M.P. is in office, encourage him or her to join the Canadian branch of Parliamentarians Global Action (PGA), a world-wide network of legislators working to advance the common security agenda in their own parliaments and at the United Nations. The Canadian Chairman is Hon. Walter McLean, M.P., Special Envoy for U.N. and African Affairs.

24. How many military bases and defence plants are in your community? Find out. Visit them. Learn what their value is, in terms of jobs and revenue. Discuss with community leaders what will happen if, as a result of disarmament negotiations and shortage of money for defence budgets, these bases or plants close. Examine what military conversion is all about, so that your community can continue to grow even if defence spending is cut. Write for conversion material to Project Ploughshares, Institute of Peace and Conflict Studies, Conrad Grebel College, Waterloo, Ontario, N2L 3G6.

25. Ask a drama group to produce *A Walk in the Woods,* a Broadway play about two Soviet and American disarmament negotiators that explains in an amusing (but deadly serious) way why disarmament negotiations are so frustrating. Stage performance

rights are controlled by Dramatists' Play Service, Inc., 440 Park Avenue South, New York, N.Y., 10016.

26. Make it a family priority to learn about other cultures. There are many multi-cultural dolls available. Try ethnic menus.

27. War toys are a problem for parents who want to shun violence. Quietly inform family members and friends that you would prefer non-military toys as gifts for your children. But if you banish a military toy, you may cause resentment and cut off an avenue of discussion with a child. Sometimes it's better to use the war toy as an object of discussion.

28. Make a habit of watching the evening TV news with your children and discussing current events over dinner.

29. Talk to your minister or priest about more sermons on peace and social justice issues. Visit a friend's church and find out what's being done there.

30. On November 11, most communities honour the war dead. Attend such services and pay your respects to those who fell in defence of our country. Ask the organizers beforehand if your group could take part in the ceremony as part of the celebration of peace.

31. Organize special events (seminars, media presentations) around other special days in the peace calendar: Mother's Day, (originally created to protest war), August 6 and 9, Hiroshima and Nagasaki Days, October 24, United Nations Day. The latter falls within the annual Disarmament Week, which provides scope for sustained community treatment of global issues. Try an art show in a shopping mall.

32. The U.N. World Disarmament Campaign has diverse written and visual material available for all interest groups and ages. Write Department for Disarmament Affairs, Secretariat Building, Room 3100A, United Nations, New York, N.Y., 10017. While you're thinking about the U.N., subscribe to *U.N. Chronicle,* a monthly journal that will keep you up to date on U.N. activities.

33. If your family visits Ottawa, (and many do to see the new National Gallery and Museum of Civilization as well as the Parliament Buildings) visit the War Museum. It's a sombre and educating experience.

34. Ask your local school principal what is being taught on the environment, world development and nuclear weapons. Judge for yourself if your child is getting the appropriate education for life in the 21st century. Has a U.N. Model Assembly ever been held in your child's school?

35. Work to develop a peace curriculum and get it adopted by your school board. Gather information on curriculum developments across Canada from The Canadian Peace Educators Directory, P.O. Box 839, Drayton Valley, Alberta, T0E 0M0.

36. Encourage your child to develop a pen pal with someone in the Soviet Union. The Canadian Embassy in Moscow or the Soviet Embassy in Ottawa will provide the link. Probably the Soviet child is learning English and will want to practice. It might be an incentive for your child to learn some basic Russian.

37. Pop music and rock videos are dealing more and more with global problems. Listen to the words. Let your children know that you are listening.

38. The Canadian Committee for Five Days of Peace works to establish five-day ceasefires in war zones throughout the world in order to immunize children. Do you want to help? Write: 170A Booth Street, Ottawa, Ontario, K1R 6P1.

39. Sports events can make important contributions to peace. The Communications and Culture Branch of External Affairs has an International Sports Relations to Olympic Co-ordination section which engages athletes as goodwill ambassadors. Find out about this innovative approach.

40. Join international groups, such as Beyond War (4484 West 11th Avenue, Vancouver, B.C., V6R 2M3) and Better World Society (1100 Seventeenth Street NW, Suite 502, Washington, D.C., 20036) which run education and media campaigns to mobilize an international constitutency dedicated to securing a sustainable future for the planet.

41. Visit an Eastern Bloc or Third World country. Read up on the country beforehand. Talk to local people and get *their* views (you have to journey beyond the tourists' beach for this).

42. Donate money to a development, disarmament or environmental NGO. You'll get a tax receipt. Remember, while these organizations need money, peace needs your active involvement.

43. On the subject of money, protest against government cutbacks in official development assistance. If you don't, the poor of the developing countries are going to get less help from the developed countries.

44. Invite eight to ten people of different backgrounds to your home for an evening of discussion. Start out with a leading question: "What do you really think of Gorbachev?" The discussion will be interesting. Who knows what more ideas than I've listed here will emerge?

45. On New Year's Eve, take five minutes to toast peace, and resolve to develop a more urgent attitude to your role in building global security.

SUMMARY

Agenda for the 1990's

An extraordinary moment in world history has arrived. The Cold War that has so poisoned relations between the United States and the Soviet Union since World War II is ending just as a recognition is taking hold that global problems of the arms race, world poverty, environmental degradation and staggering debt can only be solved by new international partnerships. The dramatic actions of Soviet leader Mikhail Gorbachev symbolize this new potential for peace. World attention is riveted on him. What Gorbachev is saying is no different than the leading edge of international thinking for the past decade. But he has created a new climate. The world can now move forward to a new system of common security in which international peace would rest on a commitment to joint survival through structures to manage the planet – except for an old obstacle.

Standing as the biggest block to global progress is the strategy of nuclear deterrence, which paralyzes true progress in disarmament. Nuclear deterrence is a fatally flawed policy and must be replaced by a new global security system as called for by the United Nations. The nuclear arms race can be ended, global development can proceed, the destabilizing disparities in the world can be corrected if we seize this unique moment and move the world towards the total elimination of nuclear weapons. A recommended agenda for the 1990's, leading to the goal of common security, includes:

- Stop the modernization of nuclear weapons;
- Implement a Comprehensive Nuclear Test Ban Treaty as an essential measure to save the Non-Proliferation Treaty;
- Eliminate all short-range nuclear weapons in Europe;
- Reduce U.S.-USSR stocks of strategic nuclear weapons to minimal deterrence – no more than 500 on each side;
- Help *perestroika* to succeed by integrating the Soviet Union into all world economic systems;
- Achieve conventional force balance in Europe by huge reductions;
- Complete multilateral negotiations for a ban on the production of chemical weapons.

- Institute annual meetings of the U.N. Security Council at the summit level;
- Create a U.N. "global watch" centre to monitor the potential for regional conflict by the accumulation of arms, economic and social disparities and environmental destruction;
- End the paralyzing Third World debt crisis by comprehensive international action by governments and commercial institutions;
- Develop world-wide cooperation for sustainable development.

Canada, which used to have the reputation as one of the most progressive countries in the world, must move to the forefront of this new wave of history – not just the government but also the people as a nation of concern and action. Just as the less powerful people in a democracy are called on to limit the excesses of the most powerful, the less militarized societies bear a special responsibility in bridling the global war system. Bold steps by the Canadian government are required:

- Oppose all nuclear weapons modernization, thus ending permission to the U.S. to test in Canada all cruise missile delivery systems;
- Work for a Comprehensive Test Ban Treaty by supporting the forthcoming international conference to amend the Partial Test Ban Treaty;
- Press both superpowers to reduce their nuclear weapons to minimal deterrence;
- Insist that NATO adopt a policy of no-first-use of nuclear weapons;
- Make the Canadian Arctic a nuclear weapon-free zone;
- Expand the peace-keeping ability of the Canadian Forces as a major contribution by this country to global security; end the token presence in Europe of Canadian troops when East-West conventional force reductions are implemented;
- Use Canadian experience in verification issues to lead the international community to a U.N verification agency;
- Publish policy outlines on common security and assign a special parliamentary committee to conduct public hearings across Canada;

- Promote conversion plans in which, as disarmament moves ahead, the workforce and industrial base of military spending are converted to the production of goods and services in the civilian sector.

Non-governmental organizations in Canada are well established and play a vital role in raising public consciousness in disarmament, development and environment issues. But they must reach beyond the already committed and make an impact on all the main avenues of society. Creative new steps are needed:

- Form a coalition of disarmament, development and environment groups to start Project 2000, a plan to mobilize public support for common security policies by a series of national meetings throughout the 1990's;
- Expand global education efforts through media, university, school, church and community bases;
- Increase the role of women in peace and development work by facilitating their participation in decision-making processes.

Notes on Sources

For wider reading on the themes addressed in this book, I note the following.

Chapter 1   The 1980's: How the Arms Race Produced World Crises

Out of the large body of literature on nuclear deterrence, I have drawn from the writings of Michael McCGwire, senior fellow at the Brookings Institute; the 1987 report of the U.N. Secretary-General, Study on Deterrence (U.N. document A/41/432); the book by John Finnis, Joseph Boyle and Germain Grisez, Nuclear Deterrence, Morality and Realism (1987); and my own 1984 Kelly Lecture at the University of St. Michael's College, Toronto, Beyond Nuclear Deterrence: A Global Challenge to Politics, Law and Religion. I have also drawn on the article by David Cox, "Arms Control Magic . . . Less is More," Peace & Security, Summer 1986, pp 2-3. There are also many publications describing the cumulative impact of the arms race. I have used principally two expert studies done for the U.N. Secretary-General: Climatic and Other Global Effects of Nuclear War (A/43/351) and Economic and Social Consequences of the Arms Race and Military Expenditures (A/43/368); also World Military and Social Expenditures 1987-88 by Ruth Leger Sivard. Sources for data are the 1989 yearbook of the Stockholm International Peace Research Institute; Strategic Survey 1987- 88, published by the International Institute for Strategic Studies; the Arms Control Association, Washington, D.C.; Nuclear Free Seas, a briefing report published in 1989 by Greenpeace; the 1989 report of the United Nations Children's Fund, The State of the World's Children and The State of World Population 1989 by Dr. Nafis Sadik, Executive Director, United Nations Population Fund. Throughout the book, I have drawn from the The Gaia Peace Atlas, 1988, and State of the World 1989, A Worldwatch Institute Report on Progress Toward a Sustainable Society. Global fiscal figures are in U.S. dollars; thus, annual global military spending of $1 trillion amounts to $1.2 trillion (Canadian).

Chapter 2   The 1990's: Disarmament, Development, Environment Action

To describe the importance of the Non-Proliferation Treaty, I have drawn on documents issued by the NPT Review Conferences and the report of the 55th Pugwash Symposium, held in Dublin, Ireland, May 5-7, 1989. An excellent set of recommendations on the Comprehensive Test Ban problem is contained in Phasing Out Nuclear Weapons Tests, a report of a meeting Sept. 29–Oct. 1, 1988, of scientific, political and legal experts on nuclear testing under the chairmanship of former U.S. Secretary of State Cyrus R. Vance and New York attorney Adrian W. De Wind. Richard L. Garwin, of IBM Research Division and professor at Columbia and Harvard, provided me with helpful papers. In discussing development, I have used my own book, Justice Not Charity: A New Global Ethic for Canada; the Barbara Ward Memorial lecture given in New Delhi, India, March 26, 1988 by Maurice Williams, Secretary-General of the Society for International Development; Development for People: Goals and Strategies for the year 2000, edited by Khadiya Haq and Uner Kirdar, published in 1989 by the North South Roundtable; the 1989 report of the Development Assistance Committee of the Organization for Economic Cooperation and Development: Development Cooperation in the 1990's; the article, "South-North Danger," by Ivan Head, published in

Foreign Affairs, Summer 1989; and numerous journals. The final consensus statement of the 1987 International Conference on the Relationship between Disarmament and Development is, in my view, a landmark document. The most complete treatment of environmental problems and prospects is Our Common Future, the report of the World Commission on Environment and Development. Other material on the environment includes the final statement of the 1989 Interaction Council Meeting on "Ecology and Energy Options"; the summary statement of the U.N. Conference on Sustainable Development, Oslo, 1989; and the vivid presentation "It's a Matter of Survival," by David Suzuki on the CBC five Sundays, July 16, 23, 30 and August 6 and 13, 1989. The final statement of the Government of Canada conference, June 27-30, 1988, in Toronto: The Changing Atmosphere: Implications for Global Security succinctly outlines a course of action.

Chapter 3   2000 and Beyond: The Road to Common Security

The selected bibliography provides the publishing information on the Brandt and Palme reports. In addition, I have used the Final Statement of the Palme Commission, issued in Stockholm April 14, 1989. Robert Johansen's article, "Global Security Without Nuclear Weapons," published in Alternatives XII, 1987, is an excellent analysis. Lynn H. Miller's Global Order: Values and Power in International Politics is a scholarly treatment of the rise and decline of the nation-state. The Conquest of War: Alternative Strategies for Global Security by Harry B. Hollins, Averill L. Powers and Mark Sommer is a guide book on the application of common security. Minimal deterrence is discussed in Robert McNamara's book, Blundering Into Disaster. The summary of Proceedings of the Structures for Peace convocation in Washington, D.C. in 1989, which I attended, convey the commitment of an important group of non-governmental leaders to the common security issues.

Chapter 4   The Soviet Union: Gorbachev at Centre Stage

The vignette in the opening paragraph was provided to me by a senior official in the Soviet foreign ministry. Gorbachev has outlined his thinking in his two books, A Time for Peace and Perestroika: New Thinking for Our Country and the World and his seminal article in Pravda and Izvestia Sept. 17, 1987, "The Reality and Guarantees of a Secure World." His 24-page speech to the U.N. General Assembly was given Dec. 7, 1988. The Soviet resolution on comprehensive security and the voting patterns are contained in U.N. Document GA/7814, January 16, 1989. The quotations from and references to George Kennan are taken from his article, "After the Cold War," in the New York Times Magazine, Feb. 5, 1989 and his testimony to the U.S. Senate Foreign Relations Committee, April 4, 1989. I have also drawn from his book, The Nuclear Delusion. John Battle, of the Harriman Institute for Advanced Study of the Soviet Union at Columbia University, provided me with writings resulting from his most recent tour of the Soviet Union. I confirmed Battle's findings on shortages of consumer goods, especially food, during my most recent visit to the Soviet Union in 1988. The paper, "Present Realities vs. Future Possibilities," prepared by Marshall D. Shulman, Professor Emeritus of International Relations at the Harriman Institute, for the Second Niels Bohr Symposium, Copenhagen, May 18-23, 1989, was also helpful.

Chapter 5   The United States: Old Ideals Needed

President Bush's policies on Soviet-American relations and arms control and disarmament were contained in speeches May 12, 1989 at Texas A&M University and May 24, 1989 at the United States Coast Guard Academy, New London, Conn., and in a letter to other Western leaders prior to the NATO Summit, May 29, 1989. A copy of American Agenda was provided to me by the Center for Defense Information, Washington, D.C. Several issues of The Defense Monitor in 1988 and 1989 contain analyses of U.S. defence spending in the Reagan years, as do recent issues of the Bulletin of the Atomic Scientists, published by the Educational Foundation for Nuclear Science, Inc., Chicago. The references to "Discriminate Deterrence" are taken from the Gaia Peace Atlas, p. 176. The 1988 U.S. voting record at the United Nations is contained in U.N. Document GA/7814, January 16, 1989. The report of the Committee for National Security, New Thinking in Soviet Defence Policy; New Opportunities for U.S. Arms Control Initiatives, was provided by one of its authors, former U.S. Ambassador James F. Leonard, who was also a member of the Palme Commission. As an example of the current thinking of disarmament advocates, I have drawn from a paper, A Paralysis of the Imagination – the Military Policy of the Bush Administration, by Michael Klare, Associate Professor of Peace and World Security Studies, Hampshire College, Amherst, Mass., and David Callahan, author of From Dawn Until Dusk: Paul Nitze and the Cold War, provided by Sane/Freeze International, New York, N.Y. The McCloy-Zorin Agreement was published in the Bulletin of the Atomic Scientists, February, 1983. The influence of defence spending on the U.S. economy is found in Norman Cousins' The Pathology of Power, cf. pp. 158-164. Paul Kennedy treats the long-range effect of U.S. defence spending in his book, The Rise and Fall of the Great Powers, cf. pp. 514-540.

Chapter 6   Canada: Boldness Required

The 1987 Defence White Paper, Challenge and Commitment: A Defence Policy for Canada; the 1986 Hockin-Simard Report of the Joint Committee on Foreign Policy; the report of the Consultative Group on Disarmament and Arms Control Affairs, Agenda for the 1990's; the report of the Group of 78, Canada and Common Security: The Assertion of Sanity are primary documents. An analysis of cruise testing in Canada is contained in Communiques Nos. 59 and 60, February, 1989 of the Canadian Centre for Arms Control and Disarmament. I have used the 1988 Review of the North-South Institute and Roger Hill's article, "Unified Canada-U.S. Defence Production: A Hazardous Road," in Peace and Security Summer, 1989. I have also drawn from the article by Ernie Regehr, Project Ploughshares Research Coordinator: "Canada and Disarmament: An Agenda for the 90's," published in Ploughshares Monitor, June 1989. The Swedish government provided me with a copy of "A Policy for Disarmament and Development." Discussion papers on debt and East-West relations by Parliament's Committee on External Affairs and International Trade were helpful. The views of the Canadian Government and summaries of the Parliamentary debate on defence, arms control and disarmament issues can be found in the yearly editions of A Guide to Canadian Policy on Arms Control, Disarmament, Defence and Conflict Resolution, published by the Canadian Institute for International Peace and Security.

Chapter 7   China and India: The Paradoxes Revealed

The policies of the Chinese government on disarmament are published in China and Disarmament, issued by Foreign Languages Press, Beijing, 1988. The Richard Nixon quotation is taken from the former President's article on China, published in the Globe and Mail, Toronto, June 26, 1989. Prime Minister Rajiv Ghandi's address to the U.N. Third Special Session on Disarmament is published in U.N. document A/5-15/PV.14, June 15, 1988. A thorough discussion of India's and Pakistan's nuclear preparations is contained in the Bulletin of the Atomic Scientists, June 1989. pp. 20-26.

Chapter 8   The United Nations: The Decline of Military Alliances

Three recent speeches by U.N. Secretary-General Javier Perez de Cuellar, in addition to his annual reports, give a sense of direction for the future of the U.N.: a lecture at the New York Public Library, April 12, 1988; the Nobel lecture given in Oslo, Norway, January 9, 1989; an address to the International Relations Club, Warsaw, May 4, 1989. The two-year study on the future of the U.N., conducted by UNA-USA, is published in A Successor Vision. The UNA-USA president, Edward C. Luck, and Tobi Trister Gati, UNA-USA vice president for policy studies, published an article, "Gorbachev, the United Nations, and U.S. Policy" in the Washington Quarterly, Autumn, 1988. I have also drawn from a paper by James S. Sutterlin, "The Objectives, Requirements and Structure of a War Risk Reduction Centre within the United Nations," given at the Conference on the Establishment of Multilateral War Risk Reduction Centres, Warsaw, April 24-25, 1989. The U.N. publication The United Nations at Forty (1985), is a helpful document.

Chapter 9   Energizing the Political Process

I have drawn from my own article on the peace movement in Canada, published in the Canadian Encyclopaedia (Hurtig, 1988). The material in Breakthrough, a publication of Global Education Associates in the Spring/Summer 1987 edition devoted to "Educating for a Global Future," was helpful. Peace Education News, a quarterly publication of the Canadian Peace Educators' Network, is a good source of information on Canadian education developments. Introducing: The World, A Guide to Developing International and Global Awareness Programme, (Reford-McCandless International Institute, Toronto, 1985) is a valuable handbook. The ATA Magazine, published by the Alberta Teachers' Association, devoted the May/June 1989 issue to "Global Education."

Chapter 10   The Ethical Basis of Change

The first three volumes of Ethics and International Affairs (1987, 1988, 1989), published by the Carnegie Council on Ethics and International Affairs, provide a wide range of discussion of this subject. A thorough discussion of the ethics of nuclear deterrence is contained in Nuclear Deterrence, Morality and Realism by John Finnis, Joseph Boyle and Germain Grisez. Pope John Paul's position on nuclear deterrence is stated in his message to the U.N. Second Special Session on Disarmament; the World Council of Churches' position is in Gathered for Life, the official report of the Sixth World Assembly; the Canadian Catholic position is in "Global Justice: Global Peace," a statement by the Canadian Conference of Catholic Bishops and other Catholic organizations.

Chapter 11   The Role of Women in Peace and Development

Women and Arms Control in Canada, by Maude Barlow in collaboration with Shannon Selin and published by the Canadian Centre for Arms Control and Disarmament, provides a succinct treatment of the subject. The Directory of Women in Canada Specializing in Global Issues is published by the Canadian Council for International Cooperation. The State of World Population 1989 report is devoted to the topic "Investing in Women." The Nairobi conference's Forward-Looking Strategies for the Advancement of Women is published by the U.N. (Document E.85.IV.10). UNIFEM's 1988-89 report is entitled "Strength in Adversity: Women in the Developing World."

Selected Bibliography

BOOKS

Barnaby, Dr. Frank, (ed.), (ed.), *The Gai Peace Atlas,* Doubleday, New York, 1988

Brown, Lester R., *State of the World 1989,* W.W. Norton & Co., New York, 1989

Catrina, Christian, *Arms Transfers and Dependence,* Taylor & Francis, New York, 1988

Cohen, Maxwell and Margaret E. Gouin (eds.), *Lawyers and the Nuclear Debate,* University of Ottawa Press, 1988

Cousins, Norman, *The Pathology of Power,* W.W. Norton & Co., New York, 1987

Dyson, Freeman, *Weapons and Hope,* Harper & Row, New York, 1984

Finnis, John, Joseph Boyle, and Germain Grisez, *Nuclear Deterrence, Morality and Realism,* Clarendon Press, Oxford, 1987

Fromuth, Peter (ed.), *A Successor Vision: The United Nations of Tomorrow,* University Press of America, Lanham, Md., 1988

Goodwin, Geoffrey (ed.), *Ethics and Nuclear Deterrence,* Croom Helm, London, 1982

Gorbachev, Mikhail, *Perestroika: New Thinking for Our Country and the World,* Harper & Row, New York, 1987

Gromyko, Anatoly and Martin Hellman (eds.), *Breakthrough: Emerging New Thinking,* Walker and Co., New York, 1988

Haglund, David G., and Joel J. Sokolsky (eds.),*The U.S-Canada Security Relationship,* Westview Press, Boulder, Colo., 1989

Hollins, Harry B., Averill L. Powers and Mark Sommer, *The Conquest of War,* Westview Press, Boulder, Colo., 1989

Keating, Tom and Larry Pratt, *Canada, NATO and the Bomb,* Hurtig Publishers Ltd., Edmonton, 1988

Kennedy, Paul, *The Rise and Fall of the Great Powers,* Random House, New York, 1987

Matthews, Robert O., and Cranford Pratt (eds.), *Human Rights in Canadian Foreign Policy,* McGill-Queen's University Press, 1988

McNamara, Robert S., *Blundering Into Disaster,* Pantheon Books, New York, 1986

Melman, Seymour, *The Demilitarized Society: Disarmament and Conversion,* Harvest House Ltd., Montreal, 1988

Miller, Lynn H., *Global Order: Values and Power in International Politics,* Westview Press, Boulder, Colo., 1985

Newhouse, John, *War and Peace in the Nuclear Age,* Alfred A. Knopff, New York, 1989

Nye, Joseph S. Jr., *Nuclear Ethics,* The Free Press (MacMillan),New York, 1986

Peringer, Christine, *How We Work for Peace,* Peace Research Institute, Dundas, Ont., 1987

Regehr, Ernest and Simon Rosenblum (eds.), *The Road to Peace,* James Lorimer & Co., Toronto, 1988

Rhoder, Richard, *The Making of the Atomic Bomb,* Simon and Schuster, New York, 1986

Roche, Douglas, *United Nations: Divided World,* NC Press Limited, Toronto, 1984

Trudeau, Pierre E., *Lifting the Shadow of War,* Hurtig Publishers Limited, Edmonton, 1987

REPORTS

Brandt, Willi, *North-South,* MIT Press, Cambridge, Mass., 1980

Brundtland, Gro Harlem, *Our Common Future,* Oxford University Press, New York, 1987

Haq, Khadija and Uner Kirdar (eds.), *Development for People: Goals and Strategies for the Year 2000,* North South Round Table and UNDP, New York, 1989

Palme, Olaf, *Common Security: A Blueprint for Survival,* Simon and Schuster, New York, 1982

Index

Other Books by Douglas Roche:

United Nations: Divided World

A Fast paced examination of the need for, and role of, the United nations today amidst the global crises of the nuclear arms race and economic development.

Written in a popular style for the concerned citizen, this book offers an objective view of the United Nations – what it has done, and some compelling recommendations on what it must do if humanity is to survive. Canada's "bridge building" role is outlined both in terms of our own commitment to the U.N., and how we are viewed by its major groupings. Dealing with the UNESCO situation, he urges the United States to stay in the controversial agency. "The U.S. and other western nations must fight to extend their democratic values."
160 pages / 5.5x8.5 / ISBN 0-920053-28-9 / $9.95

Politicians for Peace

"The effort of some parliamentarians to halt this march and bring this world back to sanity is told by Roche, who is known as a champion of third world development." – *The Ottawa Citizen*

An exciting look at *Parliamentarians for World Order*, where individual parliamentarians are taking the initiative.
224 pages / 6x9 / ISBN 0-919601-89-8 / $9.95

What Development Is All About

It plunges past the headlines into the real story of Canada's billion dollar aid programme. Some projects hinder development in the poorest countries – and Canada makes a net profit in its relations with the top ten recipients of our bilateral aid.

Roche challenges us to re-examine where aid money is going and raises questions about our own concepts of human development.
172 pages / 5.5x8.5 / ISBN 0-919601-44-8 / $9.95

ORDER FORM

Building Global Security ISBN 1-55021-057-2	$14.95	_____
United Nations, Divided World ISBN 0-920053-28-9	$9.95	_____
Politicians for Peace ISBN 0-919601-89-8	$9.95	_____
What Development Is All About ISBN 0-919601-44-8	$9.95	_____
	Shipping and handling	__$2.00__
	TOTAL $	_____

Check one: ☐ cheque payable to NC PRESS LIMITED

☐ VISA   Number _____

☐ MasterCard   Expires: ____/____ Issued: ____/____

Signature _____

Name (please print) _____

Address _____

City _____ Prov./State _____ Code _____

Mail to: NC Press Limited, Box 452, Station A, Toronto, ON, Canada M5W 1H8